Classroom Survival Skills – Creating a Laughable Classroom

Humor Me...
I'm A Teacher

Linda Henley-Smith

D0942970

Educational Cyberconnections Inc.

Educational Cyberconnections Inc.
1225 East Broadway, Suite 230
Tempe, AZ 85282

Liberty of Congress Cataloging-in-Publication Data

Henley, Marilynn D., Ph.D. & Bolster, Sharon J., Ph.D. Jan 2000
      Humor Me...I'm A Teacher / by Linda Henley-Smith

      ISBN: 1-92955-05-7

Project Editor: Cindy Daniels
Contributing Editors: Sharon Bolster, Marilynn Henley
Design Editor: Nancy Thorne
Graphic Design Artist: Erika Diehl
Word Processing: Ronda Zerbe-Carlisle
Printers: Crown Press
        Print Partner

Printed in the United States of America

PREFACE

Recently, The Wall Street Journal, reported that 8% of the 275 employers responding to a recent survey said that they discourage humor in the workplace, 8% include "fun" as part of their mission statements and 63% were neutral about the importance of humor. Only four percent of the respondents had hired a humor consultant. Are we fostering a "humorless" society?

As long-time teachers we have associated and worked with thousands of teachers throughout the years and have come to develop and appreciate a good sense of humor! After all, kids give us fresh fodder for laughter each day and what day doesn't go by that inspires us to smile, snicker, laugh, giggle or guffaw out loud at our own attempts to communicate, understand, or "deal with" our students? Ah yes, these precious youngsters are the joys of our lives. Sometimes, however, they have conflict, tension, and anger in their lives that erupts in the classroom. These eruptions can cause disruptions that cause us to grumble, growl, and grimace. It is during those times when we really need to remember the power of humor and laughter and have the tools ready to turn negativity into positive energy.

This book, "Humor Me... I'm a Teacher" will help you do just that - keep the positive energy in your classroom flowing. This handbook offers suggestions and ideas for transforming your classroom into a better and happier place where learning and growing come more easily and naturally. So, sit back, read and savor this book. We know you will find this hilarious and enjoyable book an asset to your teaching.

Still laughing after all these years,

Marilynn Henley and Sharon Bolster

FOREWORD

LAUGHTER IS A FUNDAMENTAL PART OF A FUNCTIONAL CLASSROOM

If you are a teacher, congratulations! This book is for you. It's a guide to help you reawaken your playful, spontaneous self. It's designed to help you dig up your funny bone that may have been buried for a while under the paper work, lesson plans, and assorted teaching duties.

You have chosen to guide children into adulthood. You probably did not become a teacher for the high financial rewards you reap. You are an educator because you want to prepare children for the future. You want to touch their lives and maybe provide them with the tools necessary to meet challenges and find success in the world.

What an opportunity! But teaching isn't easy. Everyone knows that being a teacher means dealing with runny noses, dirty hands, pushing, shoving and crying...and that's just in the teacher's lounge. Dealing with the children is a whole other ball game.

Trying to effectively communicate and teach without humor is about as successful as nailing Jell-O to a wall. Laughter is a highly motivating teaching tool. It only makes sense that when children are enjoying what they are learning, they will retain that knowledge. It isn't necessary to teach in a clown nose or moose antlers, unless you want to, but a little lightheartedness goes a long way toward making the classroom environment one that is conducive to learning and retaining knowledge.

Every teacher has lived the nightmare of trying to add a little levity to the lesson and having the kids go crazy. This causes the teacher to lose control, scream, and more than likely punish the entire class...which certainly defeats the original purpose of adding a little humor. After experiencing this once or twice, the teacher usually adopts the "Bah Humbug Attitude," vowing to never again bring laughter into the classroom.

You may be afraid that using humor will distract and disrupt, or possibly undermine your authority. Actually, the opposite is true. Well-placed humor will enhance the classroom experience and add to your effectiveness.

With so much violence in our schools, we need to provide children with alternatives to anger and aggression. By creating a laughing classroom, we are demonstrating that we can take our work seriously and still take ourselves lightly. Children benefit from examples more than from lectures. They often take their cues from us. If we send a message that w-o-r-k does not have to be an unpleasant four-letter word, children will have a better attitude toward schoolwork.

Laughter is the gift that keeps on giving. It is the great communicator, motivator, and healer…and it just makes you feel better!

Laughter is the best medicine. What better gift to give to our students than the gift of mirth. When our children learn to laugh at themselves and are encouraged to look for the joy in life, they are learning that there are alternatives to anger, aggression, and abuse. When they learn to laugh with each other, they are developing one of the most valuable life skills they can possess. Of course, they must also be made aware of one caveat: we must always use humor sense in our sense of humor. That means being aware of people's sensitivities. Humor can be an effective way to reach someone; but if it makes us seem insensitive to another's needs, it is not appropriate.

Teachers know that children respond to laughter. They are more receptive and retain more information when lessons are presented in a light and humorous fashion. Statistical data will support that theory, but anyone who has ever stood in front of a classroom full of children doesn't need statistics!

As teachers, we have a chance to make a difference in the lives of children. We know that our attitudes are contagious and that we set the tone of our classroom. Children will usually live up to our expectations. If we create an ambiance that is conducive to creative and fun learning experiences, we can expect students will meet us on that level. If children come into a classroom and meet a teacher who sends a message of dullness, drudgery and despair, . . . they may respond in like manner.

On these pages, you will find exercises for students and teachers. Each one is designed to help create an "attitude of altitude" in your classroom. Teaching will either cause you to crack up or crack you up. The decision is yours. Remember: Laughter is not taught . . . it's caught!

"If you're afraid to get your chest wet, you'll never get to ride on the waves." age 9

LIFE 101: HOW WELL ARE WE PREPARING OUR STUDENTS?

PROBLEMS AS CHALLENGES

The patterns of traditional classroom teaching have changed throughout the years, but for the most part, the message to students has largely been that the teacher talks and they listen. There is a time for study and a time for play and never the twain shall meet.

Although we teachers may often feel that this is the time-honored and most effective method of classroom management, we would do well to consider the value of utilizing humor techniques to teach communication skills, cooperative learning and appropriate social interaction that are grounded in "real world" contexts.

Anyone who has spent any time living has probably learned that if you are having a life with no problems, you are not having a life! It is important to send a clear message to children that life won't always be perfect and sometimes it's not even very fair. That is not the same thing as teaching them to expect the worst, but a little realism doesn't hurt. The fact is, everything doesn't always go the way we would like.

What we want our young people to understand is how to adjust their attitudes and raise their altitudes. This means that we want them to learn to view any situation that troubles them as a challenge, rather than as a problem. There is a difference in those two viewpoints. When an event is viewed as a problem, it becomes a barrier. If we adjust our attitudes and consider it as a challenge, a troublesome situation can become a learning experience.

We have the obligation to teach our students that they ultimately have dominion over their lives. We all have the right to do those things that are life-enhancing and uplifting. Our children must recognize they are stronger than anything that stands in the way of them achieving their self-empowering goals. This means when peer pressure rears its head, and a child is tempted to go along with some destructive behavior to avoid rejection, he or she must feel it is acceptable to take advantage of other options. We can help our kids by arming them with the power of alternatives and choices. This will help them to achieve an attitude of altitude.

PRACTICE DURING "PEACETIME"

Rather than waiting until a challenge occurs and then trying to teach alternative choice management skills in the heat of a crisis, we should discuss and reaffirm these ideas with our students in "peacetime." It is advantageous to conduct exercises that encourage them to entertain positive decision making thoughts to resolve conflict. Creating hypothetical conflict-based scenarios and allowing the kids to role-play and talk through possible reactions and resolutions is one way to foster creative solution-oriented thinking. If we teach and encourage positive thinking as an alternative to violent behavior in conflict resolution, we will be helping our students to set life-long conditioning patterns. They will begin to condition themselves to choose an attitude of altitude and avoid slipping into a habit of non-productive negativity.

Negative attitude can be addictive, just like a drug. It permeates our lives and destroys hope. It is true that misery loves company. Sometimes, negative people tend to gravitate toward others who share their joy of groaning and moaning. Negativity tends to manifest itself in other addictions, which can keep us in that eternal downward spiral. A wonderful legacy to pass on to our children is a spirit of worthiness and empowerment. This gift is bestowed through the consistent nurturing of habitual positive focus. A sense of humor is an integral part of the process.

Michelangelo was once asked how he could possibly create such extraordinarily beautiful pieces of art out of lumps of rock and stone. He answered by saying the beauty and the art were already there in the stone. He needed only to chip away the excess pieces to reveal the masterpiece. What a wonderful metaphor that is. All we need to do is to chip away the excess pieces of remorse, anger, fear, guilt and all the other negative emotions that inhibit a sense of peacefulness.

CHANGES IN BUSINESS

In today's world, businesses are looking for employees who possess more than academic skills. In order to be successful, candidates for employment must demonstrate the ability to work as a team with diverse people, communicate clearly and function in a variety of social and business situations. Most importantly, they must be able to face challenges with a cool head and a sense of humor. If children are going to grow up to meet these criteria, we must begin now to teach them to choose their battles and not sweat the small stuff.

We must guide them and build their coping skills so that when life presents a speedbump, they can easily glide over it. The word *humor* is derived from *umor*, meaning fluid. That's what humor allows us to do; be loose and go with the flow. If we can teach kids to move away from negativity and choose to deal with problems using positive and creative solutions, we will have instilled in them a lifelong pattern of coping with challenges in a positive way rather than resorting to anger, substance abuse or violence.

In the business world, employers are beginning to realize that when employees are given a comfortable and lighthearted work environment, there is less absenteeism and more creativity and productivity on the job. Likewise, when children enjoy a comfortable, secure and fun classroom environment, they tend to miss less school and become more active in class participation.

CHANGES IN CLASSROOMS

The word *paradigm* is often overused, but it is a good one to describe some of the positive changes taking place in many classrooms today. Educators are using multiple strategies to help children develop critical thinking and collaborative skills.

Creating a "fun"ctional classroom goes a long way toward preparing our children for dealing with life's challenging situations. Stress management, attitude adjustment and the ability to be creative in analyzing and solving problems are important tools in coping in the adult world. We need to develop and pursue goals beyond academics for our students. Teaching them to "think out of the box" is one of the greatest gifts we can bestow as we guide them in developing lifelong learning patterns.

In reading this book, keep in mind the results that are possible by interjecting some humor skills into our curriculum. For instance what if . . . . .

➢ We focused on creating an enjoyable, fun and lighthearted environment in our classrooms?

➢ We taught children how to value their individuality and develop their unique senses of humor?

➢ We sent the message to our students that having fun and learning are not mutually exclusive?

➢ We created a student-centered classroom, allowing our students to actively participate in the learning process?

➢ We helped our students to achieve an attitude of altitude?

The laughable classroom promotes

➢ Motivation
➢ Creativity
➢ Productivity
➢ Self Esteem
➢ Positive interpersonal relationships
➢ Cooperative learning techniques
➢ A strong sense of teamwork
➢ Communication skills
➢ Constructive problem solving skills
➢ Positive social interaction

A "fun"ctional classroom fosters the blessed and life-saving characteristic of resiliency. When children learn to laugh and appreciate the joy in any given situation, their chances of becoming a survivor increase. Most of us have witnessed the phenomenon of two people who find themselves in the same tragic situation; in which one not only survives, but also thrives and the other crashes emotionally and carries the defeat forever. The difference may well be in how each person has learned to deal with negativity and crisis.

Resilient people seem to share some basic characteristics. They have a highly developed concept of social competence, a strong sense of self-esteem, a sense of hope for the future, the ability to creatively solve problems, and a healthy sense of humor.

If the sound of hearty laughter is a common one in your classroom, you will know you are helping to provide your students with a healthy learning environment.

In ancient times, a king decided to find and honor the greatest person among his subjects. A person of wealth and property was singled out. Another was praised for his business acumen. Many other successful people were brought back to the palace and it became evident that the task of choosing the greatest would be difficult.

Finally, the last two candidates stood before the king. They were a little old woman and a little old man. They both had hair of white and wore the lines of age on their faces. Their eyes shone with the light of knowledge, understanding and love.

"Who are these people?" asked the king. "Why are they standing amongst the greatest minds of my kingdom?"

The king's aide answered, "You have seen and heard the others. These are their teachers." The people applauded and cheered and the king came down from his throne to honor them.

---Anonymous

THE TEN HUMOR COMMANDMENTS FOR TEACHERS

I   Thou shalt be responsible for thine own happiness.

II   Thou shalt use humor to deal with stressful situations in thy classroom.

III   Thou shalt seek and find humor in everyday life and create for thy students a peaceful place of learning wherein laughter abounds.

IV   If thou has problems dealing with difficult people: rather than raising thy voice at the offenders, thou shalt humor them.

V   Thou shalt visualize positive images and convert negatives into positives.

VI   Thou shalt regularly exercise thy soul with laughter.

VII   Thou shalt allow thyself and thy students indulgence in creative silliness.

VIII   Thou shalt keep in touch with thy child within and teach thy students to value their own whimsical creativity.

IX   Thou shalt never use inappropriate humor.

X   Thou shalt mentor thy students in laughter and impart to them the value of joy.

ASK PROFESSOR IMA HOOT

Professor Ima Hoot

Dear Professor Ima Hoot:

I seem to have a problem letting go of my inhibitions and laughing in public. I feel I will not be taken seriously as a professional if I allow myself to act silly and light-hearted. I am also afraid to let humor into my classroom because I'll lose control of the class. Is there any hope for me?

Signed,

Feeling Tense

Dear Tense:

It sounds to me as if you are suffering from quite a walloping case of "humorrhoids." This is an unfortunate condition in which the laugher is in you but can't get out. You must rectify this immediately, as bottled up laughter will implode and cause expansion of the hips. Humorrhoids are the first step toward a much more serious disorder called Terminal Seriousness.

I recommend a rigorous regimen of light-hearted, lip loosening "laffercise." Begin by throwing your head back and howling like a coyote. As the tension leaves your body, you will begin to feel the healing energy coursing through your system. Howling loosens the humorrhoids, thus clearing a path for the laughter that is buried deep inside of you.

Now, standing in front of a mirror, try to recall the face you used to make as a child .. you know, the one your mother said not to make because your face would grow that way. Make this face now. Stick your fingers in your face holes and stick your tongue out of your mouth. Jump up and down and make donkey noises. This may or may not make you feel better, but it certainly will entertain those around you. Chances are, however, that you will feel silly, which is healthy and the first step toward breaking down those grown-up inhibitions. One word of warning: It is probably best not to do these exercises during a staff meeting or a parent-teacher conference.

As for using humor and losing control of your classroom - if you're that tense, you have probably lost control anyway. You can't hold kids' attention if you don't have any fun with them. Take a good look at the pages of this book and perhaps you will gather some ideas that will help you to adjust your attitude and improve your "laughitude."

Sincerely,

Professor Ima Hoot

FULL ESTEEM AHEAD!

Few people would argue that healthy self-esteem makes a major difference in the quality of a person's life. Children with low self-esteem are likely to find that success in relationships and life skills is greatly reduced. The seed of self-esteem must be planted and nurtured until it takes root and begins to develop. It should be our goal to provide each child with roots and wings. Roots, to provide a strong foundation from which to grow and wings to facilitate exploration and flight.

High self-esteem is not necessarily related to family, wealth, social class, ethnicity or level of education. It is a matter of self-acceptance and it comes from the quality of relationships that exist between children and the people who play significant roles in their lives. It is a recognition of respect and worthiness, which gives children the ability to focus on themselves as valuable parts of the community and the world. When a child knows he or she is seen as an asset to the group, his or her self-image reflects this knowledge.

As teachers, we are aware that building children's self esteem should be incorporated into the curriculum. It is a cumulative process, which is a part of every day and every activity. Our goal is to instill into these children a confidence that is rooted so deeply, it will never fall out. In order for a child to experience a positive feeling in the classroom, the environment must support that attitude.

A laughable classroom is a place where every child feels comfortable and free to try new things and appreciate the joy of learning without having to worry constantly about grades. We should celebrate children's uniqueness and encourage them to look at the world through laughing eyes.

"Without love and laughter there is not joy; live amid love and laughter."

---Horace

LESSONS WE SEE

I'd rather see a lesson than to hear one any day;
I'd rather one should walk with me than merely tell the way.
The eye's a better pupil and more willing than the ear,
Fine counsel is confusing, but example's always clear;
And the best of all the teachers are those who live their creeds,
For to see a good put in action is what everybody needs.

I soon can learn to do it if you'll let me see it done;
I can watch your hands in action, but your tongue too fast may run
And the lecture you deliver may be very wise and true,
But I'd rather get my lessons by observing what you do;
For I might misunderstand you and the high advice you give,
But there's no misunderstanding how you act and how you live.

One good man teaches many, we believe what we behold;
One deed of kindness noticed is worth forty that are told.
Who stands with men of honor learns to hold his honor dear,
For right living speaks a language which to everyone is clear.

Though an able speaker charms me with his eloquence, I say,
I'd rather see a lesson than to hear one any day.

---Adapted from the poem *"Sermons We See"* by Edgar A. Guest

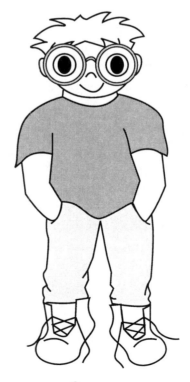

THE SEVEN MULTIPLE INTELLIGENCES

Most educators are familiar with the work of Gardner who has identified the seven intelligences that are common to all human beings. They are:

Verbal/Linguistic: Thinking and learning through written and spoken words
Logical/Mathematical: Thinking deductively; dealing with numbers, recognizing abstract patterns
Visual/Spatial: Thinking in images and pictures
Musical/Rhythmic: Recognizing tonal patterns; learning through rhythm, rhyme and repetition
Interpersonal: Learning through group relationships
Intrapersonal: Learning through working alone
Body/Kinesthetic: Learning through physical movement

In traditional classrooms, most of the learning is promoted through verbal/linguistic and logical/mathematical intelligences. Consider how many exciting concepts remain untapped in a classroom environment that doesn't include learning by use of the other basic intelligences. For instance, some children who struggle with mastery of basic multiplication facts will learn them in a flash when they are put to music. And all of the intelligences are put to use in group learning, otherwise known as the interpersonal intelligence.

One of the biggest mistakes we can make as teachers is to teach subjects in unrelated units. When we present topics independently of one another and fail to connect them, we miss out on the golden opportunity of constantly reinforcing subject matter and teaching children to integrate their knowledge into daily activities. When our students understand that every concept they learn complements everything else they have been taught they begin to see the value of the information we are presenting. It is important for educators to realize that keeping lessons contained in separate curriculum boxes can easily sabotage creativity.

All of the strategies in this book are designed to utilize the seven multiple intelligence styles to reinforce concepts and demonstrate to students how all of their bits of knowledge work together to provide problem solving and social interaction skills. It is a method of teaching which focuses on human development as well as curriculum. The best part is that the children will be learning that it is acceptable to have fun while learning in school. What a concept!

"People share more with you when you're smiling than when you're grumpy."
age 6

CREATING A LAUGHABLE CLASSROOM

When we think about humor, our minds usually focus on laughter, comedy, jokes, etc. But humor is actually a euphemism for positive attitude and the ability to appreciate the things that are funny, pleasant or uplifting.

As teacher, you don't have to plan comedy routines or constantly entertain the students. Obviously, you are in the classroom to teach; it's the attitude with which you teach that is critical. It is not necessary to be a stand-up comedian in order to create an environment that is conducive to positive feelings. Demonstrating that you have an appreciation of humor and are willing to try new things will go a long way toward creating a comfortable learning environment for your students. When students learn to laugh at themselves, they take a giant step toward learning how to handle life's challenges.

There are many ways to foster positive attitude in your classroom. Creating a totally balanced environment includes more than just academics. Try incorporating some of the following techniques on a daily basis to create a laughing classroom, which fosters unity and heightens student self-esteem. You'll find that taking yourself lightly while taking your work seriously will make you a more effective and balanced teacher and a happier person, in and out of the classroom. What's even better, is that your students will enter your classroom every morning with a feeling of excitement, and wonder. They may even begin to look forward to coming to school . . . and you will, too! The next section of this book has a variety of ways to create your laughable classroom.

ASK PROFESSOR IMA HOOT

Dear Professor Ima Hoot:

I hear of teachers who use humor in their classrooms but personally, I don't see the purpose in it. Children come to school to learn, not to have fun. They can have fun on their own time. Besides, it's important for them to realize that life is not a comedy club! What do you think of that?

Sincerely,

Responsible Teacher

Professor Ima Hoot

Dear Responsible:

I am fascinated by your attitude. You seem like the type of person who would tell a child to wipe a smile off of his face and then wonder why he wasn't listening or learning in your classroom. My advice to you is to get your panties out of a bunch!

You signed your letter "Responsible Teacher." Let's take the first part of Responsible, which is *response*. You want your students to respond to you, but that's not going to happen unless you adjust your thinking. It seems to me as if you have hardening of the attitude. You can't communicate with someone if you don't have his or her attention. Students will be more likely to listen to someone who has an appreciation for fun. An upbeat attitude bridges generational and social gaps and establishes a non-threatening environment.

For your reading pleasure, I have taken the liberty of listing some of the benefits derived from putting a little levity into your classroom:

➤ Humor creates a common bond
➤ Humor puts students at ease
➤ Humor boosts morale and builds self esteem
➤ Humor promotes teamwork
➤ Humor gives students the freedom to be creative
➤ Humor allows us to break away from routine thinking
➤ Humor motivates
➤ Humor heals
➤ Humor enhances productivity
➤ Humor offers an alternative to aggression and anger
➤ Humor provides perspective. It allows us to stand back and look at a situation more clearly
➤ Humor establishes an attitude toward life, which will result in mastery over life's challenges

I hope, for your sake and your students' that you will remember that a sense of humor doesn't make everything better for us, but it certainly makes us better for everything!

Sincerely,

Professor Ima Hoot

Enjoying a "fun"ctional classroom begins with creating an environment that fosters feelings of high self-esteem in each individual student. This is enhanced by a strong sense of class unity. Such an ambiance can be achieved through the use of activities and classroom set-up such as the ones below, through which students are encouraged to work together in the spirit of fun and positive attitude. As a teacher, you set the tone of your classroom. Try some of these classroom mood elevators and remember that your attitude is contagious.

CLASS GOAL QUILT

(A great way to start a semester or term)

Materials: **Squares of paper**
                 Crayons or colored pencils

This is a team-building exercise that will foster a sense of community and the physical result will serve as an inspiration throughout the school year. It is a great semester starter, but can be used anytime.

Ask each of the students to think of a goal that he or she would like to accomplish during the year. It should be something that is really important to the student and it may or may not have anything to do with school. Instruct them to decorate their squares of paper, using designs, words or symbols to represent their goals. Have them sign their names in the corner of the paper.

After everyone has finished, invite each student to share his or her goal and then place them all together in the shape of a quilt, on a bulletin board or a classroom wall. Throughout the year, remind the students to encourage each other in pursuing their goals. When someone achieves his or her goal, a class celebration might be in order. The quilt should remain in view as a reminder that we all need something towards which to work.

WACKY BASKETS

A little touch of the theatrical never hurts and can certainly spice up a lesson . . . particularly if the subject matter happens to be drier than a dusty day in the desert! Keep a "wacky basket" near your desk, full of random and assorted props. When presenting mathematical formulas, allow the "professor" to appear, sporting horn rimmed glasses, fake nose, and mustache, or whip out the Viking horns while teaching about Nordic history. Puppets are always entertaining communicators and can sometimes present subject matter in a unique and memorable way.

Every Wacky Basket should include a bottle of bubbles, which can serve as boredom breakers for students and teachers alike. Keep some plastic hand clappers, which can be purchased at any party store, available to give someone a round of applause for a job well done. Decorate a cardboard tube and dub it the "Talking Stick." During class discussions, whoever is holding the stick has the floor.

Add some musical instruments to your basket. Introduce a new subject with a kazoo fanfare, or strike a gong to mark the end of a class period. There is no limit to the fun you can have creating your personal Wacky Basket; and it is guaranteed that your students, no matter what age, will look forward to seeing what you have added. Surprise them with your learning props! We seem to learn faster and retain more information, when it is presented in an interesting and unique style. It will be difficult to tell who is having more fun - you or your students!

THE MAD HATTER

If you want to grab your students' attention and let them know what's next on your agenda, try adding an assortment of hats to your repertoire. Have a hat you wear when you make announcements, one that is worn when assigning homework, and another that lets the students know it's time for a play break. Soon, the students will recognize each of your hats and immediately know what is going to happen.

LAUGHTER LIBRARY

Wouldn't it be wonderful if every classroom had a special corner where students and teachers alike could retreat, regroup and "lighten up?" You can stock your laugh library with all kinds of books, tapes, magazines and word games that "edutain." Students will enjoy decorating their fun space with appropriate props and pictures. Another thought worth considering: imagine what might happen if you planned your schedule so the last ten minutes of class were devoted to sharing humor. If you have a class clown whose antics seem inappropriate during other times, this might be the ideal forum for him to try out his material. Offer three-minute "comedy spots" to budding stand up comedians. Read a funny story or challenge your students with some riddles. Instead of scrambling toward the last few minutes of class feeling rushed, frustrated and burned out, you and your students will leave with a positive feeling about the day rather than a burning desire to escape from your classroom.

GIVE YOURSELF A PAT ON THE BACK!

Another fun way to create a humorous and upbeat environment is to provide the students, and you with a way to pat yourself on the back, anytime it seems appropriate. Using a large piece of cardboard, draw and cut out a giant hand, with the palm facing out. Keep it close at "hand" so that when someone deserves a pat on the back for a job well done, or just feels the need for encouragement, you will have your hand handy to acknowledge the deserving person. This is just a silly and fun way to "hand out" praise and strokes of encouragement along with a healthy laugh.

COMPLIMENT CARDS

Unfortunately, too often, it seems as if the only time we comment on a student's behavior is when he/she has done something wrong or if he/she has accomplished something extraordinary. Sometimes, we all just need to be told that we're valuable beings just because we are unique and important individuals. If we take the time to acknowledge someone just because he/she is an important part of our classroom team and possesses worthy assets, we take great strides toward boosting self-esteem and perpetuating kindness. When a child realizes he/she is very special, even if not the smartest, strongest, or most outgoing, he/she will begin to develop confidence and a healthy attitude of self-acceptance.

Keep a stack of 5x7 cards in your desk and make an effort to distribute several "compliment cards" each week, making sure that each student receives a somewhat equal number over the course of the year. If you want to add stickers, cartoons or funny pictures to the cards, so much the better. You will be surprised at the difference it can make in a child's life when he or she receives a note from the teacher saying that his smile lights up a room or her willingness to help others is much appreciated. The compliments most certainly should be sincere, and everyone has some endearing quality; so find one and encourage the student in that area. Children become what they hear. Children will find it easier to measure up to our compliments than to stoop to meet our criticism.

Try this for a while and you may be surprised at the results. You just might find a compliment card or two in your desk from an appreciative student, whose life you touched in a positive way.

An interesting enhancement to this theme will allow you to carry the good feelings and spirit of camaraderie to your fellow teachers. Try sending a compliment card to someone on your staff who seems to be having a tough time or perhaps to someone with whom you have a difficult time relating. It may just open the door to better communication and, in any case, it is impossible to send or receive a nice note from someone and not have a smile cross your face. The compliments you give to others just might be the only ones they have received in a long time. It may make all the difference in the world to them. Even if it doesn't, you will have done something nice and that's good for the soul!

In your personal life, you might even send a funny note or a cartoon with your check, the next time you have to pay a bill. Imagine the face of the person who opens that envelope. You'll probably lighten up someone else's day, and you'll get a kick out of thinking about the utility company or the IRS representative's reaction!

"Men show their character in nothing more than by what they think laughable."

---Goethe

T.G.I.M.

We live in a society that lives for Fridays. Everywhere we turn, we hear "Thank Goodness It's Friday." This is an attitude that is being passed on to our students because, too many times, it becomes clear that teachers are just as anxious to get to the end of the week as the kids! Wouldn't it be nice if there could be a paradigm shift, which would enable us to actually look forward to the workweek?

We can create this feeling in our classrooms and our staff lounges if we adopt a conscious T.G.I.M. attitude, so that we actually make school such a pleasant place to spend time, we look forward to Monday mornings. The Monday as "Funday" movement has to start somewhere, so it might as well be with you. Begin by hanging a simple hand-made or computer generated banner in your classroom and in the teacher's lounge with the initials T.G.I.M. Once you have declared your undying enthusiasm for the beginning of the week, take steps to make sure your attitude is contagious. Bring in treats, wear a costume, pass out balloons; do anything to make Monday out of the ordinary and break the "beginning of the week blues" pattern. In your classroom, plan a special event to kick off the week; maybe a five-minute Joke Break or a mid-day popcorn party. Include your students in the planning. It doesn't have to be anything elaborate because Mondays are usually hectic and there is much to be done anyway. Just do something fun and different and use your sense of humor to set the mood for the entire week.

At first, your students and co-workers might think you've flipped your lid, but that's o.k. The best way to grab someone's attention is to step out of the lines and dare to be a little different. Soon, you'll find others picking up on your lead and quite possibly, your students and your staff might find Monday a little less mundane.

PLAN A VISIT FROM "THE LAUGHMEISTER"

Part of the secret of effective teaching is using the element of surprise. Anything out of the ordinary will be an attention grabber. A little imagination and a few minutes of extra effort can reap a bounty of results if you are willing to do things a little differently every now and again.

Imagine how much fun your students would have if they came into the classroom to find a note from The Laughmeister on each desk. Silly little riddles or one-liner jokes taken from any joke book will do, and the mood will immediately lighten as students compare jokes, try to solve riddles, and just giggle at the absurdity of it all.

Or, the laughmeister could leave footprints (made of construction paper) all across the room and over the tops of desks. The footprints could even lead to a hidden treasure of inexpensive treats for everyone in the class.

As in all the suggestions in this book, expensive or time-consuming activities are not the key. The idea is to add a little fun to the classroom and create an environment of joy and creativity. When students learn to expect the unexpected, they enter your classroom with a sense of excitement and wonder, which translates into successful learning and high self-esteem.

I SEE A CHANGE IN YOU!

Humor seems to be at its best when it's unexpected. Every now and then, surprise your students and test their powers of observation at the same time. Come into the classroom and begin your normal routine as if nothing is different. But something will be different, because you will have changed something minor about yourself. Maybe you are wearing two different color socks or perhaps you have your shirt on backwards. Don't make it too obvious, but expect the giggles as your students begin to notice a change in you.

WITH A QUACK QUACK HERE AND A MOO MOO THERE . . . .

Rather than just calling names from the roster when dividing students into groups for activities, try some new and fun techniques. For instance, ahead of time, prepare little slips of paper, one for each student, with a type of animal written on each one. If you have twenty students and you want them to be in equal groups of five, you will write "chicken" on five slips, "cow" on five slips, and so on.

Tell the students that they will have to find the other members of their group by making the noise of the animal on their paper. When they hear other "animals" making the same noise, they will recognize them as fellow group members. It is quite funny to hear the snorting, oinking and clucking going on, mixed with the giggles. You might also try this method of grouping at your next staff meeting for an extra dimension of entertainment and variety.

Another fun method for group-dividing is to make several jigsaw puzzles out of tagboard and give each student a piece. Everyone must circulate to find the other pieces that will fit together with their piece to form a complete puzzle.

ACCENTUATE WHILE YOU PUNCTUATE

Proper punctuation is a skill that must be constantly reinforced and practiced. What better way to do so than to have noisy punctuation sessions with your students. The talented musician/comedian Victor Borge used to perform a hilarious bit on this very topic. Work together with your students to create your own verbal noises to correlate with various punctuation marks; a period, for instance, could be represented by a popping of the lips.

When you feel the need to refresh punctuation skills, simply pull out a piece of literature and have the students read it aloud, punctuating as they go. You will be surprised at how proficient your pupils will become at using proper punctuation.

THE HUMAN CHESS PIECE

It is quite possible, that no matter how mesmerizing we may be, our students may sometimes get a tad weary of seeing us do the same things day in and day out. In order to spice up a lesson, try transforming yourself into a giant human chess piece. While preparing your lesson, formulate a list of questions that can be answered by the class as a whole. Tell your students that the whole classroom is a giant gameboard and you are the piece that can be moved. Ask them to help you lay out the path you will take from start to finish, in order to make your way around the board. Their answers to your questions will determine the direction in which you will move. If they answer correctly, you will move a step forward. If they give an incorrect response, you will move a step backward. For a variation, you may divide your question list into levels of difficulty, in which case sometimes you will be moving more than one space, as you see fit.

You will be at the mercy of your students, who will delight in "moving" you back and forth around the gameboard. What a fun way to reinforce facts.

PICTURE THIS!

Many adults hide from cameras, but for the most part, kids love to have their pictures taken. Use this to your advantage and play "Candid Camera" in your classroom. Snap your students at various times and post the pictures on the bulletin board for all to see. This is a great way to build class unity and all of you will have a great time remembering and laughing at yourselves in the funny photos.

MUSIC SOOTHES THE SAVAGE BEASTIES

One of the most important attitude adjustment tools you can have in your classroom is a tape player and a wide assortment of various types of music. Music can make us feel jubilant, animated and uplifted, or it can mellow, sadden, or relax us. Imagine the power we derive from this non-toxic, mood-altering drug!

Music also helps us to get in touch with our feelings; it draws us in and it conjures up diverse emotions. It can be a great stress breaker and an effective energizer. Have your students listen to a selection of music and ask them to draw what they are hearing. Tell them to close their eyes and really feel the music. Then while listening to the music have them open their eyes and draw what the music is saying to them. It doesn't have to be a picture; just a mingling of colors, if that's what they choose. Explain that they are going for an impression, rather than a picture. If the music makes them feel lively, perhaps they will feel like using sharp strokes of red. If the music brings to mind quiet memories, they might choose softer colors and more delicate lines.

"Music hath charms to soothe the savage breast; to soften rocks or bend a knotted oak."

From "The Mourning Bride by William Congreve

MUSICAL CLEANUP

If you find yourself with a classroom that appears as if a tornado whipped through it, this little trick might work for you. Children, particularly in the lower grades, love this activity. Play a recording of some energetic music. Tell the children they are to work as quickly as they can to clean up their area, while the music is playing. When the music stops, they are to freeze in mid-motion and stay that way until the music starts again. Continue this game until the clean-up is complete and your room is sparkling once more.

"When something makes you feel sad, just play with your puppy."
age 5

NEGATE THAT NEGATIVITY

Discipline is a major problem in our schools today. We have all had "problem students" who have presented many challenges. We can learn much from these students, however, because they are often full of playfulness, that has been misdirected. Often times, these behavioral problem children are simply reacting to the lack of spontaneity and stimulation in the classroom. Teachers have reported that when more fun and play was incorporated into the classroom, behavioral problems diminished proportionately.

In every classroom, there will be times when tempers will flare, frustration will surface and negativity will prevail. Sometimes the antidote to that toxic atmosphere lies in a little silliness. By the way, the word *silly* comes from the Old English *saelig*, which was a blessing for complete happiness. People used to wish this for each other, knowing that total health is more than merely the absence of physical illness. So, the next time a naysayer tells you you're being silly, accept it as a compliment! When the temperature in your classroom rises, try one of these bad mood busters.

The trick to using humor in conflict resolution is to shift attention away from the problem and then refocus. A person cannot entertain anger and amusement at the same time. So, if the angry one is made to chuckle, the hostility is lessened and the direction of the situation can be altered. If an argument is escalating in one direction, humor stops it and turns it around. Humor changes expectations and reduces, resolves and prevents conflict.

ASK PROFESSOR IMA HOOT

Professor Ima Hoot

Dear Professor Ima Hoot:

I am having a terrible year. It seems as if I have all of the school's problem students in my class. I have a few kids who are constantly fighting and I can't seem to find any way to bring peace into my classroom. I am at my wit's end. I have never seen so much negativity in one place. I have tried every form of discipline imaginable. Can you help me?

Sincerely,

Ready to Throw in the Towel

Dear Towel:

It is always difficult to deal with negative people. Everyone brings joy into your classroom . . . some when they enter and some when they leave! Seriously, just remember that there has to be a reason why your students are behaving the way they are. Many times we become so concerned about disciplining that we don't spend enough time trying to figure out the reasons for the behavior. Negativity always comes from fear. Perhaps the difficult student is going through tough times in his/her personal life or maybe he or she is fearful of something about which you know nothing. Try looking a little deeper into what's really ticking inside of these kids.

In the meantime, remember that the key to defusing negativity is redirection. You must take a situation that is heading to a place you don't want it to go and redirect the energy behind it so that it takes a more positive turn. Humor is a great way to do this. Some people are not comfortable with using a humorous approach to negativity, so if that is the case with you . . . you'll need to redirect your own thinking and be willing to try something new. Sometimes changing your own attitude is the key to reaching others. It isn't about telling jokes, it's a matter of using whatever methods you can to lighten the mood and provide a comfortable and secure environment. Once you have done that, you can begin to redirect the energy, stand back and wait for the positive results.

Don't throw in the towel yet . . . as Kurt Vonnegut said, "Laughter and tears are both responses to frustration and exhaustion. I, myself, prefer to laugh since there is less cleaning up to do afterward." You might find the perfect opportunity to reach your troubled students on a level you might have never even imagined. Keep in mind that there is more than one way to look at most things. Copy this run-on sentence and use it as a motto for your classroom:

OPPORTUNITYISNOWHERE

Jestfully Yours,

Professor Ima Hoot

SCARF JUGGLING

Anyone who has ever watched someone juggle has been amazed by the professional juggler's ability to balance a chainsaw, a bicycle, and a kitchen sink and keep them all up in the air at the same time without having one item drop down and render the performer unconscious!

Juggling does not have to be complicated, but it is mentally therapeutic since the activity takes intense concentration. It is difficult to think about anything else while trying to keep everything up in the air. That is why it is such an effective way to redirect negative thinking. If you have a student who is out of sorts, caught in a negative cycle and generally in need of a mental shakedown, put him or her into the corner and let the juggling begin. Now it is not recommended that you encourage your students to juggle objects of any weight. Scarves are a good choice because they are so light, they stay up in the air for several seconds before they float back down to be caught. Another plus is that they definitely will not cause damage if they land on a head or two. It is not difficult to master scarf juggling. Most magic stores stock scarf-juggling kits, complete with step-by-step directions and a set of starter scarves. A few minutes of secluded scarf sailing will provide the juggler with the opportunity to focus on something other than his/her anger. Scarf juggling is a fun and effective way to defuse negativity!

You might keep a supply of scarves on hand in the teacher's lounge. You'd be surprised at how people's scowls turn into smiles as they try to keep the filmy little fabric pieces floating in the air. As teachers, we have to juggle lesson plans, meetings, paper work and assorted problems. Learning how to juggle scarves just might help us to channel our energies in a positive direction and clear our minds to deal with the bigger problems.

SMILE WHEN YOU SAY THAT!

There will be times, in every classroom, when conflicts between students will occur. As teachers, part of our responsibility is to provide our students with options in conflict resolution.

The "Smile When You Say That" method of problem solving was actually developed by a junior high student who was tired of watching two of his classmates swing at each other whenever opinions differed. At one point, when the two boys were nose to nose and toe to toe, ready to use the fists, this enterprising young man challenged them to say one nice thing about the other person before throwing the first punch. All of his classmates cheered at the suggestion. The perspective fighters were so surprised by the idea, they decided try it. (Besides, all of their classmates were waiting to see if the two would rise to the occasion.)

The two of them stood staring at each other, trying to think of something nice to say so they could begin the fight. It didn't take long for them both to burst out laughing and the tension was immediately released. From that point on, the students delighted in chanting, "Smile when you say that" whenever tempers started to flare.

REFRAME THIS SITUATION

When a problem is looming or a sticky situation just won't go away, sometimes we need to look at things in a slightly different way. Much like reframing a picture, we can reframe our problems. If a student just can't seem to shake a foul mood or there is a conflict between a few classmates that needs to be resolved, you can add a little levity to the situation, and teach a lesson in attitude adjustment at the same time. Keep an oversized picture frame close at hand for reframing those negative situations. When the need arises, ask the person with the problem if he/she thinks the situation merits reframing. Ceremoniously place a frame around the students' face. Ask the students to suggest an alternate and perhaps better way to look at the situation. This should break the tension and open a dialogue about problem solving and attitude adjustment. For a variation on this theme, purchase a toilet seat to use as a frame. This always gets a laugh and kids get a kick out of being "framed."

"Remember: ANGER is just one letter short of DANGER"

WHINERAMA

In every classroom, there is bound to be a certain amount of whining. Sometimes it comes from the students and sometimes from the teacher. When there is too much whine flowing in your classroom, rather than to ignore it, focus on it and allow everyone to revel in the misery.

Have the students stand up and on your signal, whine their hearts out. The louder and more irritating the whine, the better. Everyone should try to outdo each other, and that includes the teacher.

After about a minute of this, everyone should be laughing louder than they are whining.

"Everybody's gotta have their laughin' place."

-----B'rer Fox

STOMP ON YOUR PROBLEMS

Materials: Paper and pencils

This little mirthquake will encourage a fun and healthy outlet for frustrations. Announce that everyone will have a chance to "stomp on his or her problems." Have each person write down something that is bothering him/her and on your command, everyone throws down his or her paper and "stomps on their problems." This always results in gales of laughter and by the time everyone has finished stomping, all negativity and frustration has been defused and everyone is ready to continue on with the day. Pass the trash basket and have everyone ceremoniously throw their problems away.

GRUMBLE GRUMBLE

Here is another brain-breather exercise designed to provide an opportunity for release of tensions and to encourage students to vent negative feelings in a harmless way. Pair up the students and instruct them to talk simultaneously, sharing any complaints, reservations, resentments, worries, gripes or problems they have on their minds. When each student runs out of issues to disclose, he/she is to loudly say, "Grumble Grumble" until all participants are done. Call a halt to the exercise when it is apparent that the negative energy has dissipated and only superficial grumbling is present.

THE "BE" ATTITUDES

Be careful of your thoughts, for your thoughts become your words.

Be careful of your words, for your words become your actions.

Be careful of your actions, for your actions become your habits.

Be careful of your habits, for your habits become your character.

Be careful of your character, for your character becomes your destiny.

— Frank Outlaw

Attitude is contagious...would you want anyone to catch yours?

"My mom said
I need to work on
my 'gladitude.'"
age 5

FOR YOUR FUN FILES

SOME AMAZING TEACHER TRICKS
AND FUN STUFF FOR THE STUDENTS TO DO

Every teacher needs a fun file from which to pull joyful and jolly jump-starters to lift sagging spirits. Your humor resource file should be an ever-expanding survival kit full of games, jokes, funny quips and ideas on how to add some light-hearted learning into your classroom routine. Here are some boredom-busters to help you inject some much-needed levity into a humorally challenged day.

"It's bad to suppress laughter . . . it goes back down and spreads to your hips."

---Steve Allen

THE IMPRESSIVE "I KNOW YOUR AGE AND ADDRESS" TRICK

This is a fun exercise to reinforce mathematics. Ask your students to pair up with a partner. Tell them they will magically be able to guess the home address and exact age of their partner. Have each one take out a piece of paper and a pencil and instruct them to do the following:

1. Write the numerical part of their address on the paper

2. Multiply the address by 2

3. Add 5

4. Multiply by 50

5. Add their age

6. Add 365

Next, have each student share with their partner only the total of the above exercise. After each student has shown the number to another, have them subtract 615. The resulting total will give them the age (the last two numbers) and the address of the person.

Example:

Address:	1806	
Multiply:	x2	
	3612	
Add:	+5	
	3617	
Multiply:	x50	
	180850	
Add age:	+10	
	180860	
Add:	+365	
	181225	(total given to partner)
Subtract:	-615	
	180610	

Address: 1806   Age: 10

MIND STRETCHING WORD EQUATIONS

Get out your "mental floss," dust the cobwebs out of your brain, and get ready to tackle these mind-stretching word equations. Each one represents a familiar phrase or saying. Stretch your imagination and have fun.

Sugar *Please*	PERSON PERSONS PERSONS PERSONS	1 3 5 7 9 ——— WHELMING
head ache	LOV	GIVE GET GIVE GET GIVE GET GIVE GET
ALL world	INSULT + INJURY	PPOD
RASINGINGIN	GGES EGSG GEGS SEGG	HEAD SHOULDERS ARMS BODY LEGS ANKLES FEET TOES
ACUM	EMPLOY T MEN	WHOHNICLEE
wire just	COLLAR 104 degrees	DO12"OR

ANSWERS:

1. Pretty please with sugar on top
2. First person singular
3. The odds are overwhelming
4. Splitting headache
5. Endless love
6. Forgive and forget
7. It's a small world after all
8. Add insult to injury
9. Two peas in a pod
10. Singing in the rain
11. Scrambled eggs
12. Head and shoulders above the rest
13. See you in the morning
14. Men out of work
15. Once in a while
16. Just under the wire
17. Hot under the collar
18. A foot in the door

THE EQUALLY IMPRESSIVE "FUN AND SPOOKY QUIZ"

1. Pick a number from 2 to 9. It can be 2 or 9 or any number in between.

2. Take that number and multiply it by 9

3. This should give you a two-digit number. Take those two digits and add them together.

4. Take the resulting number and subtract 5 from it.

5. Correspond the resulting number to the alphabet, numbering the letters: A=1, B=2, C=3, etc.

6. Take your letter and think of a country that begins with that letter.

7. Now take the last letter in the name of your chosen country and think of an animal that begins with that letter.

8. Take the last letter in the name of that animal and think of a color that begins with that letter.

9. Good. But remember: there are no orange kangaroos in Denmark!

WACKY WORD FORMULAS

Here are some formulas to tease your brain. Relax! They are not mathematical or scientific equations. They are formulas that represent basic facts or popular sayings. Each formula contains the initials of the words that make it intelligible. Your task is to identify the missing words. For instance: 7 D=1W translates into seven days equal one week. Try some on your students. They'll love them. For an extra dimension to this exercise, challenge your students to create some wacky word formulas of their own based on subject matter you have covered in class. What a fun way to reinforce knowledge!

1. 8 P or 4 Q=1 G
2. 13 S and 50 S on the AF
3. 90 D in a RA
4. 26 A in the C
5. 24 H in a D
6. 10Y=1D
7. M+NH+V+M+RI+C make up NE
8. D+H+G+S+B+S+D are the 7D
9. 7P in the SS
10. S and H of R make up the USC
11. 360 D=the C of a C
12. 32 D F= the T at which W F
13. 8 S on a SS
14. 18 H on a GC
15. 54 C in a D (with the Js)
16. 11 P on a F T
17. 3 B M (S H T R)
18. 29 D in F in a L Y

Kids aren't the only ones who sometimes scramble their words.
Imagine the horror of this teacher as she realized how her announcement
to the drama club came out: "To begin today's play rehearsal,
I'd like to ask the boys who have small male parts to stand up."

Answers:

1. 8 pints or 4 quarts equal 1 gallon

2. 13 stripes and 50 stars on the American flag

3. 90 degrees in a right angle

4. 26 amendments in the constitution

5. 24 hours in a day

6. 10 years equal 1 decade

7. Maine, New Hampshire, Vermont, Massachusetts, Rhode Island and Connecticut make up New England

8. Dopey, Happy, Grumpy, Sneezy, Bashful, Sleepy and Doc are the 7 Dwarves

9. 7 planets in the Solar System

10. Senate and House of Representatives make up the United States Congress

11. 360 degrees = the circumference of a circle

12. 32 degrees farenheit=the temperature at which water freezes

13. 8 sides on a stop sign

14. 18 holes on a golf course

15. 54 cards in a deck (with the jokers)

16. 11 players on a football team

17. 3 blind mice (see how they run)

18. 29 days in February (in a leap year)

FUNNY FILL-INS

We all can relate to sitting in a classroom and having the parts of speech drummed into our little heads. Do we want to pass this method of learning language skills on to our poor, defenseless students? We think not!

Let them laugh while they learn language with funny fill-ins. You can reinforce knowledge of the parts of speech while the kids use their imaginations and create laughable stories. In preparation for this exercise, you can write a few paragraphs on any topic. Now, omit most of the nouns, verbs, adverbs, adjectives, etc. Do not show the story to your students. Ask them to provide you with the parts of speech you request. For instance, tell them you need suggestions for verbs to fit into your story, which you will read to them later. When they shout out their suggestions, choose the ones you feel will make the story the funniest. Do the same for the other parts of speech. When you have filled in the blank spots in your story, read it aloud to the students and wait for the laughs. Your imagination is the limit in this one!

Here is a starter story to get you going:

THE TRUE STORY OF DINOSAURS

We all know that many years ago, large
creatures roamed the _____ (noun).
Some of them had huge_____
(plural noun) and walked with _____
(adjective) _____ (plural noun)

The largest of these creatures was called
a _____ (noun) osaurus. These were
_____ (adjective) beasts who ran very
_____ (adverb) and ate
_____ (adjective)
_____ (plural noun)

Scientists have discovered that the mortal
enemy of this giant beast was the _____
(adjective) _____ (noun) osaurus. It was
the size of a _____ (noun) and the color
of a _____ (adjective) _____ (noun.) It fought with its _____ (body
part) and liked to stand on top of its prey and _____ (verb.) Anyone
who would see this huge creature would not be able to stop _____ (verb
ending in "ing")

The _____ (noun) osaurus stood _____ (number) feet high and
weighed over _____ (number) pounds. All of the toes on its _____ (noun)
pointed north and the fingers on its _____ (noun) pointed south. This
made for a very interesting sight as it ran through the _____ (geographical
location) stomping on everything in sight and smashing small _____ (plural
noun) in _____ (adverb) fashion.

It is not known how these creatures died but they probably spent too much time
_____ (verb ending in "ing") and not enough time taking care of their
_____ (plural noun.)

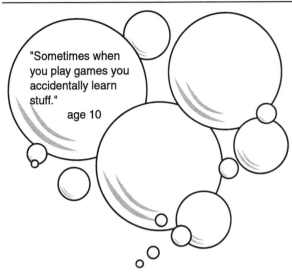

"Sometimes when you play games you accidentally learn stuff."

age 10

ENERGIZE, EMPOWER, EDUCATE AND ENTERTAIN

Creating a laughable classroom doesn't have to involve wearing moose antlers or a fake nose and moustache. A laughable classroom is one in which the students feel comfortable and secure enough to let their imaginations soar. Sometimes, when children are taught in the spirit of play, amazing streaks of genius emerge. In the laughable classroom, self-consciousness is down and self-esteem is up.

One way to incorporate laughter into your classroom is to make use of "brain-breathers" several times during the day. We can't expect kids to hang onto our every word, (mesmerizing as we may be,) for much longer than 45 minutes at a time. Research has shown that learning occurs with greater ease if instruction is divided into short time units and followed by a three to five minute play break. This gives kids a chance to "stretch their brains" just like they need to stretch their muscles after sitting for a while. Here are some tried and true brain-breathers, successfully used by real teachers, in real classrooms, full of real kids. Some of them are variations on old themes, but all of them are worth trying.

The objective of each exercise is to foster inclusion, teamwork, creativity and self-management. There are no suggested age or time limits on these exercises because they are designed to be adaptable to any group. No materials are needed unless so noted.

CONDUCTING

This is a high-energy activity that gets the blood flowing from the brain down to the feet and back up again! Select a two-to-three-minute piece of lively music, preferably without lyrics. If it begins in a slow tempo and gradually builds to a lively one, so much the better. Encourage students to imagine they are conductors of an orchestra. Tell them they may listen to the music with their eyes closed if they wish. The main point is for them to really feel the music with their entire bodies. For an added dimension to this exercise, pass around a roll of toilet paper and have each student tear off a strip the length of his or her arm. Watch the fun as these aspiring conductors wave the paper and become "in tune" with the music. When the music ends, have them give themselves a standing ovation for outstanding conducting.

ONE-MINUTE MIRTHQUAKE

On low energy days, we sometimes need a good, hearty belly laugh. If there doesn't happen to be a laugh on the horizon, we can always whip one up! This exercise is a great way for students and teachers alike to "lighten up" and shake out the cobwebs. It's simple to do. Have students stand for a moment and stretch. Then ask them to stretch their mouths into little smiles - not much - just a hint of a smile. Now have them each turn to another person and without saying a word and smile at him or her. Next, encourage them to move into the next phase of laughter, which is body movement. Tell them to tilt back their heads, slap their knees - anything that resembles a laughing gesture. Up until this time, everyone is still silent. The next step is to add noise to the laughter. Have them snort, hoot, yuck and howl. Tell them they can fake it until they make it! It's guaranteed that within a minute, the laughter will be genuine and everyone will feel better with expanded lungs and expanded minds.

GROUP DRAWING

This is a great way to encourage teamwork and to give students an idea of how different people can view a particular situation in a variety of ways. Divide the class into groups of five or six and give each group a large sheet of paper and several markers. Choose a subject and instruct the students that each member of the group will have 30 seconds to sketch his/her best interpretation of that subject. At the end of that time frame, you will indicate that it is time to pass the paper to the next person who will add his or her personal touch to the drawing, and so on. For example, you might ask them to draw their interpretation of their lunchtime in the cafeteria. Upon completion of the drawing, it will be interesting to observe and discuss what each student contributed to the total picture. This exercise is not about artistic talent; it is meant to hone students' powers of observation and shed some light on how people's perception of a situation can vary. For instance, in the above scenario, some students might focus on the social aspects, while others might be more interested in the cafeteria environment or the food.

An interesting variation on this exercise is to have the students draw a scene in a story the class has just read or studied or perhaps depict a recent field trip taken by the class. This type of group activity can be a fun way to reinforce material previously taught.

SQUEAK AND SQUAWK

This one-minute mirthquake is designed to shake out the cobwebs and reenergize after a long period of concentration. Have the students stand and shake out the kinks. Then choose someone to be the leader and have him/her stand in front of the class and make any kind of strange noise that comes to mind. A movement may accompany this noise if desired. The rest of the class is to mimic the noise until the leader decides to change the pattern, at which time the rest of the class follows suit. This sounds simple, which it is, but it is a great mental flossing activity and usually results in gales of laughter.

THE INCREDIBLE, BENDABLE CLAY PERSON

Here is a "Laugh Lesson" that will appeal to almost every age group. Although it requires the "clay person" to stand still for a short period of time, you will be surprised at how it will calm even the most "antsy" child. Students of all ages will allow themselves to be "manipulated" if it is done in the spirit of play.

Have the children pair up and choose which one will be the clay person and which will be the molder. Tell them that the clay person has absolutely no control over his/her body. The molder is totally responsible for moving the clay person's arms and legs . . . even mouth. If the molder puts the clay person's arm above his or her head, it must stay there. If the molder pulls the clay person's mouth into a frown, that's the way it has to stay.

Then tell the students you will instruct the molders to mold their clay people in various ways. You can begin by telling them to make their clay people look like the happiest people on earth. Ask them "What happens to our bodies when we are happy?" It isn't only faces that register joy; postures reflect it as well. Then continue the Laugh Lesson by encouraging them to shape their clay people to show anger, fear, surprise, etc.

"USE YOUR BEAN" BAGS

Materials: Bean bags

Here's an activity that will reinforce subject matter and can be fit into any time slot. Have a few bean bags handy so that at a moment's notice, you can toss one to a student and ask him or her a question relating to something you are discussing in class. This is a great way to fill up a few minutes between classes and before lunch. When the student answers, he or she may toss the bag to a fellow student while asking him or her another question.

TONGUE TRIPPING TONGUE TWISTERS

This brain-breather offers a quick tension breaker and is guaranteed to bring a smile to even the most stoic of faces. The exercise is done with partners and takes very little time. It's a good one for the last two minutes of the day before the bell rings.

Write three tongue twisters on the board. Tell your students that sometimes our tongues don't work in harmony with our brains. We have all experienced this at times when we can't quite get the words out. One student in the pair goes first. He/she is to read the first tongue twister four times in a row as quickly as possible. That will probably dissolve the entire class into laughter. Now the second partner has a turn, with the second phrase you have written on the board. For the final round, both partners will read the third tongue twister together as fast as they possibly can get those words out of their mouths.

SOME TRIED AND TRUE TWISTERS OF THE TONGUE TO TEASE, TITILLATE, TEST, AND TANGLE

The sixth sheik's sixth sheep's sick.

Shy Sarah saw six Swiss wristwatches.

The seething sea ceaseth, and thus seething sea sufficeth us.

Does this shop stock short socks with spots?

Three gray geese in the green grass grazing; gray were the geese, and the green was the grazing.

A skunk stood on a stump. The stump thunk the skunk stunk, but the skunk thunk the stump stunk.

WHAT IN THE WORLD ARE YOU DOING?

This is an exercise in silliness, which is sometimes just what is needed to break up routine in the classroom. Have five or six students stand in a line at the front of the classroom. The first student in line is to pantomime a simple activity, for instance, brushing his or her teeth. The next person in line asks, "What in the world are you doing?" The mimer is to respond with a silly, obviously inaccurate answer, such as "I'm swimming in my pool." The asker then takes on the role of the actor, pantomiming the action stated by the first person. In this case, he/she pretends to be swimming. The next person in line repeats the process by asking, "What in the world are you doing?" and the process continues on down the line. This is entertaining to those who are watching the activity as well as the participants. If you choose, you may have several lines working around the room, so everyone has a chance to pantomime.

WHAT CAN YOU MAKE OF THIS?

Materials: Random objects

This playbreak is a fun way to take a few minutes off from work while stimulating your students' imaginations. Have ready a few random objects, large enough to be seen by everyone in the classroom. Ask for a volunteer to come up to the front of the room and select one of the items as the object of his/her "presentation." Set the timer for thirty seconds and instruct the student that within that period of time, he/she is to come up with as many silly uses for that object as possible. Imagination is the only limit for this exercise. It is amazing how quickly minds can work when there are no restrictions. Empty paper towel tubes can become telescopes, noodle makers, unicorn horns, musical instruments, and elephant noses. Some students might feel a bit timid at first, but when the exercise is presented in a light-hearted, "there can be no wrong answers" manner, it can be a hilarious and creative experience.

WHO STARTED THIS?

Have all of the students sit in a circle and select one volunteer to momentarily leave the room. Choose one person in the circle and instruct him/her to begin making a simple motion, which can be easily imitated by everyone else in the group. An example of this might be clapping twice and then patting the top of his/her head three times. Everyone in the circle should continuously repeat this pattern. Explain to the group that the object of this exercise is to hone observation skills. Tell them when the volunteer reenters the room, they are to continue with the pattern until the leader subtly changes the pattern, at which time, they are to follow suit. The challenge is in keeping an eye on the leader without staring at him/her or making it obvious as to who is the leader. The volunteer tries to identify who is controlling the change of actions.

TOSS YOUR TROUBLES

Materials: Paper and pencils

This exercise is designed to enable students to work together to find a solution to a problem or a concern. Announce to the class that they will have an opportunity to toss away their troubles. Have students think of and write down a problem, a question, or a simple statement about something which is troubling them. They are not to write their names on the papers; all statements are to remain anonymous.

Have students crumple up the papers and toss them into a big box in the center of the room. Divide the class into small discussion groups. Have someone pull a paper from the box and read it aloud. Then give the groups an allotted amount of time to discuss the problem and work together to formulate possible solutions or answers. Each team should jot down a few solution suggestions and at the end of the time period, all the teams' solutions should be offered and discussed. This process can be repeated as time allows.

This activity teaches the students that there may be more than one effective answer to a problem and sometimes brainstorming can provide valuable insights and viable solutions. Toss Your Troubles might be better handled in small discussion groups with "problems" for one group going to another for discussion. A large group discussion could follow or summarize the solutions.

ORGANIZED THINKING

Materials: A preplanned list of 15 items in random order and a list of the same 15 items organized into categories

This is a fun exercise that can help to teach students the value of learning by association. The concept is to determine whether information is retained better when it is presented in a fashion that allows them to associate similar bits of information.

Divide the class into two groups. Tell the students that they will be asked to memorize the names of fifteen objects in a very brief time period. Let them know that the items will all be common to a particular area; for instance, they will all be household objects, items found in the classroom, or things found in a store.

Provide Group A with a sheet of paper on which is printed a list of objects in a random order. Give the members of Group B a list of the same items, but organized into specific groups.

Example: The list for Group A might read

Things Found in a Department Store

Shorts, dog leash, roller blades, underwear, birdseed, helmet, fish tank, shoes, basketball, flea collar, socks, cat-food, skateboard, bike, shirt

The list for Group B might read

Things Found in a Department Store

dog leash, birdseed, fish tank, flea collar, cat-food
bike, helmet, skateboard, roller blades, basketball,
shoes, socks, underwear, shirt, shorts

Each student is to work individually to memorize the fifteen items in an allotted period of time. When the time is up, have each student use a clean sheet of paper to list as many of the items as they can remember. Allow an appropriate length of time to do so. After that time has passed, read the list and have each student score their own papers. Compare the results of the two groups and discuss them. Which group scored higher? More than likely, it was Group A, whose items to be memorized were organized by specific groups. Talk with the students about the value of organized thinking in other areas of their lives.

SING YOUR LESSONS

This is a play break that is fun, silly and yet provides practical reinforcement of concepts. Studies show that people learn quickly when information is put to music. Consider how soon toddlers learn to sing nursery rhymes and think about how many times you, as an adult, catch yourself chanting advertising jingles! Putting facts to music is certainly not new, but you and your students will have a good time reciting multiplication tables to rap music or learning the nation's capital cities to the tune of "Yankee Doodle." Your imagination is the limit on this one and no musical knowledge is required - just an attitude that reflects your willingness to live your life in the key of laughter!

MIRROR MIRROR

This is a quick energizer that will also sharpen the students' powers of observation. Have the students pair off and stand face to face. One is the mover and the other is the mirror. The mirror must copy, in great detail, every movement and expression made by the mover. They can start out with slow, simple movements, such as the wave of a hand or the lifting of an arm and then move on to more detailed and specific actions.

CHARADES

It's hard to beat good, old-fashioned charades for a brain-breather activity. For a variation on the theme, you can have a class shout out phrases for a volunteer to pantomime. The actor should react with whatever movement comes to mind when he or she hears the phrase. Encourage creative phrases, such as "bucking bronco" or "clothes on a clothesline."

ADD-ON STORYTELLING

Divide the class into groups of five or six and instruct them to sit in a circle. Give one person in each group a "jumpstart" story starter. Pick any topic you choose, but make it one that will lend itself to some imaginative story lines, for instance, "piano-playing penguins" or "lawn mowers with wings." The first person is to begin the story, introducing the topic with only one sentence. The next person is to pick up where the first person left off, adding one more sentence to give the story more meaning. This pattern continues around the circle, with each person adding more substance and fun to the story.

WEB WEAVING

Materials: **A ball of yarn**

This is a brain-breather that will encourage the students to focus on the positive and foster a sense of community and support for one another in the classroom. All that is needed for this exercise is a ball of yarn.

Have everyone sit in a circle. Give one person the ball of yarn and ask him/her to state something for which he/she is grateful or something positive that happened to him/her during the day. While holding the loose end of the yarn ball, that person now tosses the ball to another person who will repeat the exercise. Each person, in turn, holds onto a length of the yarn and tosses the ball to another. When everyone has had a turn, the entire class will be enveloped in a web of positive feelings.

CHANGE THREE THINGS ABOUT YOURSELF

This exercise will challenge your students' powers of observation and allow them to get some of the kinks out after sitting for a long time. Ask them to choose a partner and face each other. Tell them to take a really good look at each other because soon they are going to turn back to back and change three things about themselves. Tell them they can do anything they like: take off an earring, roll up a sleeve, remove eyeglasses, or whatever they can think of. Give them about thirty seconds to do this and then tell them to turn back around and face each other again. Allow another thirty seconds for each partner to tell the other what changes they have noticed.

MOTOR MOUTH

This exercise is designed to provide students with the opportunity to stand up in front of a group to speak, without having to be under any pressure. It is a fun way to allow them to improvise and learn to feel relaxed in front of an audience.

The objective is to provide them with a topic idea and give them an allotted period of time, in which they are to speak non-stop, as quickly as possible about that topic. Choose an appropriate time frame for students, perhaps 30 seconds to one minute.

Have the class come up with possible topics and write them on the board. The first volunteer will choose one of the topics and you will start the timer. Tell the speaker that the only rule is that he/she must talk non-stop, pausing only for a breath. If the "motor mouth" runs out of ideas, he/she can make something up. The only rule is that the speaker needs to try to stay on the topic and not stray to other topics.

This is a great way to reinforce concepts being covered in class. For instance, the motor mouth could speak for one minute about a lesson taught that morning.

OOPS . . . I FORGOT THE REST

Here is another verbal playbreak that requires an active imagination and quick thinking. It is also a wonderful way to encourage the students to come up with unique ideas for a creative writing exercise.

You can begin by telling the students you are going to tell them a story. Mention that unfortunately, you happen to be a very forgetful storyteller. Tell them that when you forget a word, you will say, "Oops." Ask them to help you out when you pause, by jumping in with the first word that pops into their heads. Start out with something like this: "Once upon a Oops." The students will chime in with "time." You say, "Yes, that's right. Once upon a time there were three dogs who lived in a big Oops." The children will call out a variety of words that could fit into that sentence. You pick one and continue. "Yes, that's right. There were three dogs that lived in a big shopping mall. One day, the smallest dog wanted to buy a yellow Oops." And so on.

Explain that it is the responsibility of the storyteller to repeat what the other person has contributed, and add it to the story. The story should make sense within reason, and have a beginning, middle, and end. Give them a time limit and the story must be completed within that time.

Now, divide them into pairs and let them begin to tell the tales.

SILLY SENTENCES

Materials: Index cards on which parts of speech are written

This is a brain breather that will reinforce sentence construction and the correct use of parts of speech while the kids are having a ball. Have on hand a stack of index cards, on which you have written a variety of words - one per card. It works well to use the colored cards so you can write nouns on one color, verbs on another, etc. You should have quite an assortment of cards for each part of speech.

Pass out the cards and instruct the students to find people with whom they can join to make a sentence. Remind them of proper sentence construction and the correct use of the various parts. The sentences should make sense, but they can be silly and funny; as a matter of fact, the funnier, the better!

THE HUMAN MACHINE

This is a fun way to promote teambuilding and creativity while expending some excess energy! Ask the class if they know anything about machinery. At the very least, they will know that all of the parts must be working together in order for the machine to work effectively.

Divide the class into small groups and tell them they are each individual parts of a big machine. It is up to them to decide upon the function of their machine and what each part needs to do to make the whole thing work. Encourage them to be creative with the movements and noises made by each part. Give them a limited amount of time to create this human machine and then let each group demonstrate their creation. If you think they need a jump-start, you can assign a machine function to each group.

BUCKINGHAM PALACE GUARDS

In case students don't know about the guards at Buckingham Palace, explain that they are forbidden to talk, smile, or show any facial expression. Divide the class into two groups and have each group form a line. Have everyone stand side by side, facing a person on the opposite team. There should be about three feet of distance between the two lines.

The first person in each line must walk down the aisle formed by the two groups. He or she must remain perfectly straight-faced and make no expression whatsoever. If the person cracks a smile, he or she must go and stand in the line of the opposing team. No touching is allowed. Chances are that not many will make it down the line without cracking up. If, by some chance, the walker does complete the trip, he or she may go back to his or her original line. After everyone has walked, the line with the most people is the winning team.

SNOWBALL FIGHT

Materials: Paper and pencils

This exercise is particularly effective at the beginning of the year when the students may not know each other very well, however, it certainly can be adapted for use at any time.

Have each student write his or her name on a paper along with a little known fact about him/herself. An example might be that the person won a dance contest in the first grade or likes to collect origami animals. When everyone is finished writing, tell them to line up in two lines, one on either side of the room. Instruct them to crumple their papers into balls and on your direction, they are to throw their "snowball" to the other side of the room. Everyone scrambles to pick up a snowball and then learns something new about the person whose snowball they found. Then, each person shares his or her newfound information with the rest of the class.

TIED UP IN KNOTS

This is a fast and easy energizer that doesn't take very long, but will end up with everyone laughing and maybe even on the floor! Divide the class into smaller groups for this one. Have everyone stand shoulder to shoulder in a circle. Ask everyone to reach out and grab two other hands (not on the same person and not the hands of the people on either side of you.) Tell them to avoid crisscrossing if at all possible. Without dropping hands, they are to try to untangle so that the circle is once again complete.

SHARK PIT

Materials: **Masking tape**

This is a fun mirthquake that promotes teamwork and community spirit. It is a good one for groups of 6 to 8. Using masking tape, mark an area on the floor. Fill it with as many students as possible. Tell them the tape marks are the outline of a lifeboat. The rest of the floor is the ocean and it is full of person-eating sharks that are very hungry and looking for a bite to eat. The students' mission is to work together to line themselves up according to whatever criteria you choose; height, birthdate, alphabetically by first names, etc. They must not knock anyone into the water, because that person will surely be devoured. The first group to successfully accomplish the task is the winner.

VAROOM, VAROOM AND SCREECH!

If your classroom and logistics allow, this energizer is a popular one because it enables the students to make a lot of noise, and as teachers know, kids always welcome that opportunity. Have everyone stand or sit in a circle. Start the activity by revving up your motor and making a "varoom varoom" noise, while holding your hands in front of you, as if on a steering wheel. While the students are watching you and wondering what you're up to, keep revving faster and faster and then suddenly, pull your hand down as if you were applying a hand brake and then make a screeching noise.

Tell the students that you are all going to be race car drivers and these are the racing rules: One designated person will start his or her engine and all others will follow suit. The starter will look to his right and say "varoom varoom." The person to his right will immediately look to the right as well and say "varoom varoom" and so it will continue around the circle until it gets back to the starter who will then rev up even faster (in second gear) and so on. When things get going pretty well, at any time, any person can apply the brake by making the hand signal and saying "screech!" When that happens, the action immediately reverses direction and the person who brakes must look to his left and start things going that way. At any time, anyone can brake and screech, but each person can only brake once. Eventually, everyone will have a chance to brake and screech, but by that time, the laughter will have taken over anyway.

"The first idea that the child must acquire in order to be actively disciplined, is that of the differences between good and evil; and the task of the educator lies in seeing that the child does not confound good with immobility and evil with activity."

---Maria Montessori

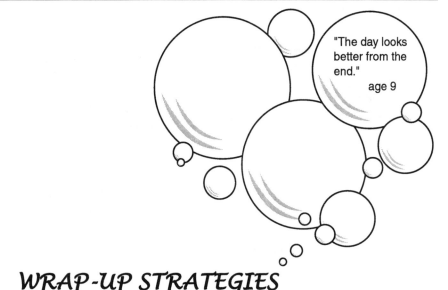

"The day looks better from the end."
age 9

WRAP-UP STRATEGIES

By the end of the school day, most teachers and students are more than ready to head out that door and as far away from school as they can possibly be. This doesn't have to be the case. Imagine what it would be like if you were able to tweak your schedule, just a bit here and there, so that rather than to end the day with chaos, you might have five or ten minutes before dismissal to "leave 'em laughing." Sometimes when students leave the classroom, their last image of the teacher is one of a frazzled grown-up shouting to them about tomorrow's homework assignment. Wouldn't it be better for all if they carried with them a mental picture of a teacher and a class enjoying each other's company with some fun? The following activities are not just time fillers, they are valuable strategies designed to build inclusion and encourage community spirit.

TEACHERS' SURVIVAL KIT

ASK PROFESSOR IMA HOOT

Professor Ima Hoot

Dear Professor Ima Hoot:

I feel constantly stressed and am overwhelmed by everything that is necessary to keep my classroom running smoothly. Everyone is so demanding! On top of that, the paperwork is killing me. People tell me I need to lighten up, but to tell the truth, the last thing I feel like doing is laughing. By the end of the day, I have a headache and absolutely no energy. All I want to do is close the classroom door and get out of there.

Sincerely,

Too Stressed to Smile

Dear Stressed:

It's true . . . teaching is not for the faint of heart! You didn't choose this career because it was going to be easy. You wanted to work with young people and teach them how to cope with life. But now it seems as if YOU need some readjustment in your coping strategies. Everyone who has ever taught understands that feeling of waiting for the final bell to ring. We've all been there! Sometimes, when the last student has left the building, we have our hands on that aspirin bottle. We might even find ourselves so fed up with the hassles of running a classroom, we long to take to heart the directive on the bottle label: "Take two aspirin and keep away from children." But we can't always keep away from children, because we are teachers and our jobs require us to stay in the classroom with them! Even if we could run away, one of them would always find us. Children are small and wiry and can squeeze themselves into small places. They can move faster than we can and they are very crafty.

Seriously, stress can take a mighty toll on a body! When you allow yourself to be caught up in the stress cycle, the adrenaline starts pumping overtime, your muscles tighten, your nervous system goes haywire and high levels of stress hormones are released into your bloodstream. You body's alarm system is going off to alert you that you are approaching a danger zone. It's no wonder you're feeling under the weather.

Just remember that stress is not an event, it is the way we perceive what is happening to us and the way we choose to react to that situation. As teachers, we have a very important responsibility and of course, must take our positions seriously. But we can learn to take ourselves lightly. In other words, everything is not a crisis. We have to learn to prioritize and choose our battles. A child stabbing a classmate with scissors is worthy of an adrenaline rush; being behind on paper grading because we have to take on an extra duty is not. One situation is potentially life threatening, the other is merely annoying. Do you see the difference?

Your students are watching you to see how you handle yourself in daily situations. They will take a cue from your attitude and the atmosphere of the classroom will adjust accordingly. If they see their teacher laughing and exhibiting a peaceful, calm reaction to minor incidents, they will respond in a similar way. However, if you are going to be a screaming ball of nerves with a look of terror on your face . . . prepare to continually enter the "Classroom of Endless Horror."

Good luck and add a little levity to your life. Try ending your day on a light note. It may take a little adjustment, but it is worth it!

Cheers!

Professor Ima Hoot

I'M SINGIN' THE BLUES

This is a fun way to share concerns in a non-threatening manner. Bring in a recording of someone singing the blues and play a bit of it for your students. Or demonstrate blues singing in a funny, over-exaggerated way. Explain to them that having the blues means feeling sad about something. Ask the students if anyone has ever had the blues and why. Using someone's example, make up a simple verse and sing or strum it to demonstrate. For instance, if a child says he is feeling sad because his pet dog ran away, your song could be, "I've got the blues. Yes, I've got the blues. I've got the doggoned, my dog is gone blues."

Ask everyone to join in the singing. It might be a good idea to first share one of your own blues. Then give the students the opportunity to lead a song about their blues. An important element of this activity is to emphasize that no one is making fun of anyone else's problems; it is just an invitation to share a concern and look at it from a lighthearted perspective.

LOOKING BACK ON THE DAY

This is a wrap-up that allows the students to calmly reflect upon the day's activities and share their feelings with others. If it has been a particularly stressful day, it helps to ease the tension so that teacher and students may all leave with a positive memory of the day.

Have the students partner with another student. If there is an odd number of students, you can be a partner. Tell them they are each to take a turn at being the interviewer. They have all seen enough television talk shows to know what that means. You may provide the students with some sample questions to ask. For instance:

➢ What was the high point and low point of your day at school?
➢ Did you have a problem with something or someone? If so, how did you handle it?
➢ Did you have a positive experience? Did someone help you or were you able to help another person?
➢ What was the funniest thing that happened today?

Remind the students to listen attentively to what the other is saying and to offer each other words of encouragement and appreciation.

THE "I SAW WHAT YOU DID TODAY" AWARDS

This strategy is actually one that begins in the morning, continues throughout the day and culminates in an end of the day wrap-up activity. It can be an on-going event in your classroom. The idea is to encourage students to condition themselves to always be helpful, kind and understanding of their classmates. Everyone likes to be recognized for his or her good deeds. This activity fosters acknowledgement of random acts of kindness.

You can make up and keep on hand a stack of "I Saw What You Did Today" award certificates. During the day, when a student sees someone extending the hand of kindness to another person, going out of his or her way to make someone feel special or simply doing his or her part to create a peaceful and enjoyable environment, that student may come to you and make a kindness report. At the end of the day, at wrap-up time, you can distribute the certificates, or better yet, allow the student who reported the good deed to make the presentation.

PUT DOWN THOSE PUT-DOWNS!

Materials: **Paper and pencils**
                  Trash can

This is an effective wrap-up activity for students of all grade levels. It goes without saying that in a group of people of any age, there will be some who will be judgmental, rude and even hurtful. This strategy is designed to sensitize the students to the harmful effects of put-downs and to promote inclusion and acceptance.

Place a large box or a trash can in the center of the room. Invite the students to write down an insult, hurtful remark or a put-down of any type that they find particularly offensive. If they have been on the receiving end of such a comment during that day, they may also write how that negative statement made them feel. When everyone has finished writing, direct everyone to make a dramatic production of crumpling or ripping the papers, thereby symbolically ridding the classroom of harmful and insensitive remarks.

LOOK AND SEE THROUGH MY EYES

Materials: **Construction paper**
                         Colored pencils or crayons

This is an eye-opening activity that can be adapted for use by different age groups. It is designed to promote understanding and acceptance of diverse backgrounds and beliefs.

Explain to the students that we all react to certain situations based upon our experiences and backgrounds. We're all coming from different places emotionally and often geographically. Although we may not always completely understand someone's belief system or behavior, it is important to acknowledge and respect the rights and opinions of others. Discuss how others' experiences often dictate their actions and reactions.

Instruct the students to draw a huge, over-sized pair of glasses. They may cut them out if they wish, although it's not necessary to do so. On the "lens" of their glasses, each person is to draw designs or symbols representing their heritage background, hobbies, family, etc. The glasses may be as detailed as they wish.

Give each student an opportunity to explain and describe his or her glasses. This way, the others will have a chance to see the world through their classmates' eyes. Follow with a discussion about how it feels when someone has a completely different view or how to deal with someone who thinks everyone should see things the same way.

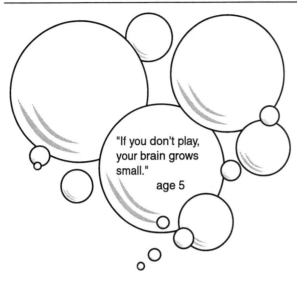

TEACHER'S PLAY PAGES

In order for teachers to be able to mentor their students in the fine art of creative silliness, they must first be willing to toss out all inhibitions and get down to the serious business of humor. Nearly all human beings realize that total health is more than just the absence of physical illness.

When we stop being "groan-up" and allow ourselves to play a little each day, we become more effective and creative in our personal and professional lives. These play pages are designed to be a reminder of how important it is to keep in touch with that elf in oursELF.

Laughter shows us that we are more important than our problems."

---Jose Ferrer

"Laughter is the shortest distance between two people"

---Victor Borge

"Real joy, believe me, is a serious matter."

---Seneca

ASK PROFESSOR IMA HOOT

Dear Professor Ima Hoot:

I try to bring laughter into my classroom. I have even noticed that I'm getting response from students whom I believed I would never reach! My problem is finding any fun in my life outside of the classroom. I live with a person who is not very uplifting. Some of the other adults in my life don't appreciate humor either. I find that when I am around them, I seem to put my funny side on the back burner. What's up with that? What can I do to lift everyone else's spirits so I can enjoy myself?

Professor Ima Hoot

Signed,

Split Humor Personality

Dear Split:

I am sorry to say that you are not alone in your dilemma. Our humor personalities don't always match up with those with whom we work or live. It can cause a black cloud to hover over our lives. Many of us wake up grouchy in the morning . . . of course, sometimes we can let grouchy keep sleeping! Ha ha . . . that was a little Hoot Humor. Anyway, the bottom line is that we are not responsible for changing anyone else's attitudes. Everyone has to do that for him or herself. We are, however, quite responsible for our own frame of mind and we have the right to feel joyful and laugh a lot if we choose. Someone else's attitude should not dictate our own.

When we are on an airplane and the flight attendant gives the preflight instruction talk, we hear about the oxygen mask that will descend if the cabin pressure drops. We are instructed to put on our own mask first, and then help anyone who needs assistance. At first thought, that sounds rather selfish until we analyze it and then it makes perfect sense. We cannot help anyone else if we are lying blue and breathless on the floor. The same holds true in our lives down here on good old terra firma. If we are emotionally distraught, we will not be able to successfully administer to anyone who might need us.

You see, dear Split, you must first don your own metaphorical oxygen mask before trying to help anyone else with his or her mask. Don't worry about fixing other people, just adjust your own attitude and keep yourself emotionally balanced. Chances are, your attitude will rub off on them because it truly is more fun to laugh than to throw pity parities.

Everyone can choose whether to live a laffenated or a delaffenated life. Keep spreading your joy to the students in your class and let the grown-ups in your life groan until they decide to live life on the laugh track.

Good Luck and keep laughing . . . it makes people wonder what you're up to!

Professor Ima Hoot

FIND THE ELF IN YOURSELF

Anyone who spends any time around children knows that they give themselves permission to have fun. When they think something is funny, everyone around them knows it. Children are constantly erupting into giggles and their laughter is contagious.

We first laugh at about two months of age. By the time we are four years old, we are laughing at the rate of about one laugh every five minutes. Then, as we mature, an amazing thing happens. Along the path to adulthood, we become too sophisticated to laugh so indiscriminately. If we were to continue on with the same fancy-free attitudes, other people might look down their noses at us, maybe even consider us "childish." Oh horror!

So, in order to fit nicely into the grown-up mold, we monitor our laughter and silliness and make sure we only display it at appropriate times, for instance, when we are intoxicated.

Because we have all read the Grown-up Handbook, we know that not only should we cease to participate in creative silliness when we hit adulthood, but we also recognize the importance of sending a clear message to the children in our lives. We must serve as role models in negativity, lest the poor little ones get the mistaken impression that growing up is a desirable thing to do!

So, we glare at them when they act silly, chastise them for goofing off and smirk as we sarcastically dish out the news that they had better have fun now, because when they grow up, they will learn what life is really about! Our very favorite thing to do to our children is to demand that they "act their age." This is particularly effective when addressing a six-year-old who is giggling and acting like a . . . six year old.

Isn't it amazing that our kids ever want to grow up? There are many adults who are bitterly unhappy and unfulfilled because they still buy into the theory that play is only for children.

GROWN-UPS OF THE WORLD UNITE! Break loose from the surly bonds of inhibition, the oppressor: lift up your heads and howl! Step away from your desk and wiggle, squiggle and do a little jig. Dislodge that stick that has been stuck you know where, and lighten up! Remember what it feels like to play, just for the sake of playing, with no competition involved.

In the best interest of your health in and out of the classroom, remember to play. If you have forgotten how, fear not because it comes back to you. In other words, find the ELF in yoursELF. Don't worry about your dignity; there is a difference between being childISH and being childLIKE. Aim for childLIKE.

The problem with grown-ups is that we tend to separate work and play. We feel that if we're having a good time while we are working, we are not taking our jobs seriously. Actually, play is an integral part of the thinking process; it breaks down mental barriers and opens the rivers of creativity.

People of all ages will be more productive if they are enjoying what they are doing. Take several play breaks during the day and never be fooled into thinking that being creatively silly is the same as being an airhead. Actually, those who take time to play are the smartest of people, because they think enough of themselves to take a break every now and then.

A recent informal study conducted at a university consisted of dividing a class of graduate students into two groups. Both groups were prepared to take a rather difficult exam, but before the test was administered, the students were told that there would be a slight delay, due to a mix-up in the scheduling of the testing rooms. The groups were sent to separate rooms to await the commencement of the exam. One group was put into a room with a television, which was tuned into a news program. They spent their time watching video footage of recent news stories, consisting of the usual . . . wars, robberies, death and destruction. The other group was led into a room usually occupied by children in a daycare program. It was full of toys, electric trains, yo-yos, bubble blowers and a wide selection of various playthings. Of course, it was hard to resist picking up those toys, so while waiting to take the test, these students played. Both groups were then given the exam and the results were very revealing. The students who had been subjected to the news program before taking the test scored 30% lower than those who had played. Why? Because negativity permeates and infects our thought processes. Laughter and play, on the other hand, fill us with a sense of well-being and positive attitude. Negativity clogs our brains and weighs us down, whereas laughter frees our thoughts and sends a message of success.

Teachers would do well to take a clue from this study. We want the best for our students and ourselves. We need to understand that people are more receptive to learning in a positive environment. Laughter allows us to disassociate and detach ourselves from a threatening situation. It is an integral step toward learning to cope with difficulties.

There is nothing juvenile about laughter and play. As a matter of fact, maturity comes with the ability to remain childlike. Play is a sign of great wisdom and insight into good mental health. It is not so much that playing lays aside the tensions of life; it is just that it moves within those tensions and creates comic relief.

In your classroom, keep high above you the banner of PLAY. Remember how empowering and healthy it is. As the actress Ethel Barrymore once said, "You grow up the day you have your first good laugh . . . at yourself!"

"We should live and learn, but by the time we've learned, it's too late to live."

---Carolyn Wells

MY LETTER TO THE CHILD IN ME

We all started out as children. At one time, the most challenging problem was what kind of candy bar to eat first. Some adults still have the same problem, but it isn't the most serious challenge they'll face in a day. Sadly, some of us become "groan"-ups. We find more reasons to complain than we find reasons to rejoice.

Would that little child you used to be want to hang out with the adult you have become? Or have you turned into a grouchy "groan"-up who has forgotten how to look at the world with a sense of wonder?

Sometimes it helps to put your thoughts on paper. Take a few minutes and write a letter to the child within you. Then, give that child an opportunity to answer. Be honest with each other. Tell each other how you really feel about your relationship.

Dear Child,

_____

_____

_____

_____

_____

_____

_____

Love,
Your Grown Up

P.S. Call me if you need me

Dear Grown-Up:

_____

_____

_____

_____

_____

_____

_____

_____

Love,
Your Inner Child

P.S. Let me out every now and then, will you? It gets stuffy in here.

Certificate of

The Right to Play and Not Be "Groan" Up

By This Certificate Know Ye That

Is a lifetime member in good standing in the Hang Onto the Elf in YoursELF Society and is hereby and forever entitled to the following:

Scratch when and where it itches; walk in the rain without a hat; jump in puddles, even while wearing dressy shoes; smell flowers; go barefoot; play hopscotch, jacks, marbles and any other game just for fun, not for competition; fly a kite; blow bubbles; act silly; dig in the dirt; wear colorful clothes; color in coloring books; read children's books; buy toys to keep at the office; sing on the way to work; stay up late; play on swings; climb trees; do nothing; look at the stars; find shapes in the clouds; daydream; eat without worry about calories; tell stories; smile at people; learn something new just for fun; dance; try a new hairdo; refuse to worry about tomorrow; decorate with things that don't necessarily match, just because they're fun; play with a child; visit a friend; learn to say "no" to demanding people; and practice things that bring more happiness, health, fun and laughter to life.

Furthermore, the above named certificate holder is officially entitled to pull his or her panties out of a bunch and laugh and play "jest for the health of it."

THE "TIGHTEN UP AND DIVE OR LIGHTEN UP AND THRIVE" HUMOR QUOTIENT ASSESSMENT

MULTIPLE CHOICE

1. Where does joy come from?
   a. a dishwashing liquid bottle
   b. the wearing of too-tight underwear
   c. from your soul

2. When your inner child surfaces, do you . .
   a. say, "Who are you and what are you doing in my psyche?"
   b. beat the daylights out of him/her for acting childish
   c. welcome and embrace him/her with open arms

3. Who said, "I like children . . . well done."
   a. anyone who has ever lived with or taught them
   b. the Galloping Gourmet
   c. W.C. Fields

4. When faced with a stressful situation, do you . . .
   a. find that your head spins around and you spit up pea soup
   b. pretend you are a Star Trek character and transport yourself to another planet
   c. try to focus on the positive aspects of the challenge

5. What do you do for fun?
   a. recite meditations and mantras of misery
   b. pull the wings off insects, kick dogs and intimidate small children
   c. anything that lifts your spirits and keeps your mind focused on the positive

6. What is your favorite form of exercise?
   a. making mountains out of molehills
   b. carrying a grudge
   c. anything that gets those endorphins pumping

7. The last time you really smiled was . . .
   a. when you had a popcorn kernel stuck in your back molar
   b. when you got a toothpick wedged sideways in your mouth
   c. this morning when you woke up and looked in the mirror

8. Is the most negative person in your school:
   a. your principal
   b. your co-worker
   c. yourself

9. Which is your attitude about playfulness and toys?
   a. any adult who plays with toys is an idiot with no respect for the true seriousness of life
   b. you play with your kids' toys in the closet when no one is watching
   c. you have an assortment of playthings at all times for easy access in times of stress

10. Which of the following most accurately reflects your attitude about laughter in the classroom?
   a. you would rather have a root canal with no anesthetic than to allow your students to laugh within the walls of your classroom
   b. you had fun once and got over it
   c. you believe laughter heals, connects, motivates, liberates, bonds and promotes teamwork, creativity and an ambiance that is conducive to learning

Scoring: Don't score number 7 because there is no right answer. For every other question, give yourself 7 points for each "c" answer. If you received 100 points, you are either fibbing or lousy at math, because it isn't possible to score 100. However, if you scored 63 points you can feel light hearted and carefree because you probably have a pretty good idea of how to put things into perspective and enjoy life. If you scored any fewer, you need to start learning how to live a laughing life.

"I am absolutely certain that being happy is what keeps you young;
and laughter helps you to do that.
You have to find out what makes you happy and just hope it's legal."

---Phyllis Diller

HUMOR INVENTORY

1. What is the most fun you've ever had?

   _____

   _____

   _____

2. What do you consider your greatest achievement?

   _____

   _____

   _____

3. How much humor was used in your home when you were growing up? What do you remember about it?

   _____

   _____

   _____

4. When is the last time you have played, just for the sake of fun . . . not just to win? When is the last time you bought a goofy toy for yourself . . . not for your kids but for you?

   _____

   _____

   _____

5. Draw a circle below. Consider these five categories: work, family, spiritual, other obligations and playtime. Divide the circle into five parts, showing proportionately how much of your day you spend on each of the categories.

How much time did you allot for your playtime? Is that satisfactory to you? If not, why isn't it more of a priority?

_____

_____

_____

_____

6. If you were to learn you had only a year to live, what would you do differently?

_____

_____

_____

_____

7. List some of the things that cause you great stress and tension during the school day. Next to each one, jot down a few humor techniques you could possibly use as stress busters.

_____

_____

_____

_____

_____

_____

8. If you are hesitant or unsure about using humor in your teaching, ask yourself why that is the case. Were you hurt by humor at one point in your life? Do you feel these techniques will cause you to lose control over the students? Write your thoughts about these questions.

_____

_____

_____

_____

_____

9. Think back on some of the teachers you had as a child. Recall the ones who made you feel enthusiastic about coming to school. What do you remember about their teaching styles and the ambiance of their classrooms?

_____

_____

_____

_____

10. Recall a time when you lost your cool with your students. Analyze the situation and, in retrospect, think about how you could have defused the negativity in a humorous way.

_____

_____

_____

_____

11. To fully understand the value of humor in building a child's self esteem, sometimes it helps to use specific, personal examples. Reflect on the students in your class. Think particularly of the ones who are challenging. Think not only about **how** they misbehave but also **why** they act that way. Experiment with some ideas on how a few humorous and light hearted methods might go a long way to boost self esteem and improve attitude.

_____

_____

_____

_____

12. How would you like to be remembered by your students? Ten years from now, if you were to receive a letter from one of them, what would you like it to say?

_____

_____

_____

_____

_____

_____

POST THIS AS YOUR DAILY "TO DO" LIST

1. Do something nice for myself

2. Take my work seriously, but myself lightly

3. Say at least one kind thing to another person today

4. Record the positive things that happen today

5. Get rid of my big "But" (I'd be happy, but...; My life would be better, but...: etc.)

A LITTLE CRAZINESS PREVENTS PERMANENT INSANITY

➢ Make your teacher's lounge a fun place to be. Decorate with over-sized inflatable chairs, funny pictures, toys, and props. Equip it with a "Joke Jar." Everyone brings in at least one joke per week to contribute. When anyone is having "one of those days'" and needs a lift, a quick dip into the joke jar will help to brighten the mood.

➢ Designate one corner of the lounge as a "Teacher Time Out" section. Have stuffed animals to cuddle with and a small Walkman with relaxation tapes available for a quick retreat.

➢ Adopt a secret pal program. Participants draw names from a hat and over the course of a month, anonymously provide his/her secret pal with inexpensive little trinkets, funny cards, etc. Secret pals' identities are revealed at a staff "Pal Party."

➢ Tape a long piece of bulletin board paper along one wall in the lounge. Keep markers or crayons nearby for people to display their humorous side through art. This is a healthy way to vent frustrations before going back into the classroom.

➢ Have everyone on the staff bring in a baby picture. Put all pictures on the bulletin board in the office and let people guess who they are. One you've seen your principal or co-worker as a chubby little cherub, you may never view them quite the same way again. This is also a fun activity for your students.

➢ In the lounge, lay in a supply of games, toys, puzzles, funny books, etc. Let stressed teachers enjoy a "recess" at breaktime.

➢ Cut out cartoons and cut off the captions. Put them on the bulletin board and have people write their own humorous captions.

➢ Once a month, have a staff theme day. Example: A Wild West Day when people dress in western clothes, western music is piped into the lounge and any willing "pardners" can bring in food for a Prairie Potluck.

➢ If there is a community pet peeve or something that bothers everyone, for instance, a bothersome district policy, make a likeness of it and use it as a dartboard in the lounge.

➢ Start a humor newsletter featuring brief stories of humorous goings-on around the workplace.

➢ Create a Doodle Corner in the lounge. Keep it supplied with paper, markers, crayons, coloring books and scissors.

➢ Start a "Magic Fingers Fund" and have everyone contribute spare change as they pass through the lounge. Once a month, use the money to hire a professional masseuse to give ten-minute shoulder and neck massages.

➢ Designate one day a week to be "No Whining Day." Anyone heard griping, complaining or whining can be fined a quarter to be put in the Magic Fingers Fund.

➢ Create a humorous glossary of teaching terms to post in your lounge. Be creative and let people add to the list. Some examples might be: "Sub"- What you have time to take one bite of on your ten minute lunch hour. Or, "Early Retirement"- What most teachers want to do at 4:00 in the afternoon after a hectic day.

"When you lose your sense of humor, you lose your footing."

---McMurphy in "One Flew Over the Cuckoo's Nest"

ADD LIGHT YEARS TO YOUR LIFE WITH LOUNGE LAUGHTER

*Here are some joyful additions to the "crazy corner"
of your teacher's lounge.*

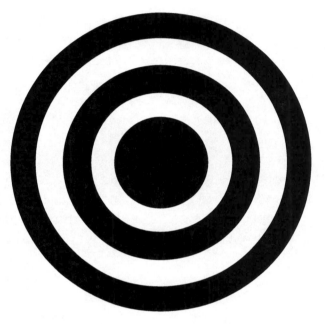

Stress Zone
Bang Head Here

YOU WOULDN'T BELIEVE WHAT I DO FOR A LIVING!

Sometimes, when we don't think we are being appreciated, when it seems as if no one fully and completely understands the services we provide and the hardships we bear, it helps to vent our frustrations. A touch of humor never hurts either.

To help others more effectively grasp what teachers do, have some fun and rewrite your job description. Tell it like it really is. Write what you and only you know to be your responsibilities. For instance, most people might think of you as a teacher. You know you are more than that. You are a doctor, a psychologist, a friend, a counselor, a substitute parent, a fix-it person, a remover of paste in children's hair, a finder of lost items, a wiper of noses, a dryer of tears and a keeper of pet worms and other items that find their way into your classroom via children's pockets. You have the capability of doing seventeen things at once, while preventing twenty-five bodies from squirming out of control. You can staple, cut, fold, correct, explain, inspire, intercede, support, and love - day in and day out. In addition to that, you possess the amazing ability to consume doughnuts and five cups of coffee while running off papers on the copy machine before class begins and the sheer willpower and the steel bladder which enables you to keep that coffee in until class is over!

Be creative, have some fun and blow off some steam.

"If a doctor, lawyer or dentist had thirty people in his office at one time, all of whom
had different needs, and some of whom didn't want to be there
and were causing trouble, and the doctor, lawyer or dentist, without assistance,
had to treat them all with professional excellence for nine months,
then he might have some conception of the classroom teacher's job."

--- Donald D. Quinn

MY JOB DESCRIPTION

_____

_____

_____

_____

_____

_____

_____

_____

_____

_____

_____

_____

_____

_____

_____

_____

*"My father worked for the same firm for twelve years. They fired him. They replaced him with a
tiny gadget. It does everything my father does, only it does it much better.
The depressing thing is my mother ran out and bought one."*

---Woody Allen

IT COULD BE WORSE

It's Murphy's Law - just when we think things can't get any worse, they do! So, we may as well count our blessings and be grateful for what we have. This is a fun exercise designed to help turn a negative into a positive by laughing at the situation.

On the lines below, write your five "peskiest" pet peeves . . . those things that cause you to gnash your teeth, snarl and generally lose your cool. Then, let your creativity and your sense of humor kick in as you come up with some way the problem could be worse! Write it on the line next to each item you have listed; for example, the problem is you have 35 students in a classroom designed to accommodate 25. But it could be worse: You could be trapped in an elevator with all of these kids!

MY PROBLEM IS: BUT IT COULD BE WORSE:

1 _____   _____

2 _____   _____

3 _____   _____

4 _____   _____

5 _____   _____

"Things are going to get a lot worse before they get worse."

---Lily Tomlin

"The greater part of our happiness or misery depends on our dispositions and not on our circumstances."

---Martha Washington

MOVE OVER STEVEN SPIELBERG!

Think of a situation that is causing you great annoyance or even distress. It seems like the biggest problem imaginable today, but in a couple of months, you'll probably be telling it as a humorous anecdote. When you really stop to think about it, your life plays out like a movie. There is humor, tragedy and all the elements of a great screenplay. You don't always have control over the situations; in other words, you may not be the producer, but you can always be the director! Go ahead! Rewrite your own script. Choose whomever you want to be the star and play "you." You can add as much glitz and glamour or pathos and passion as you wish. Anything goes. Ready?
Lights . . . Camera . . . .Action!   Roll 'em!

MY LIFE

By _____

Starring _____ as _____
                                                              (your name)

Scene 1 _____
                  (choose the scene you'd like to rewrite)

Rewrite: _____

_____

_____

_____

_____

_____

_____

_____

_____

_____

"Life is a tragedy when seen in close-up, but a comedy in long-shot."

---Charlie Chaplin

CLOSE YOUR EYES AND ENERGIZE WHILE YOU VISUALIZE

When it seems as if there is nowhere to go to escape the craziness of your world, take heart and remember the one place you can retreat where no one else can invade: your imagination. There, you can visualize life the way you want it to be. You can see, touch, hear, taste, and smell anything your heart desires. You can even re-create yourself.

Take a few minutes to close your eyes and go on a mini-vacation in your mind. Energize, empower and enlighten yourself. Let the child in you guide you in your imagery as you expand the limits of your creative thinking. Find another part of you that you have misplaced since you've been a grown-up. Create a new identity for yourself, which represents the creative and adventurous side of you. You will emerge a much more relaxed and light-hearted person. You will also find you are a more effective teacher as you guide your students in the exploration and expansion of their own imaginations.

Have some fun with this idea. Create an imaginary alter ego using the most creative thoughts you can muster. Maybe you have an amazing superhuman ability. Perhaps you smell like the desert after the rain and taste like chocolate. Don't be afraid to pretend. You just might find a side of yourself you really like!

GET IN TOUCH WITH THE "OTHER" YOU

My other name is_____

Using the five senses, I would describe myself in this way:

I look like _____

I smell like_____

I feel like_____

I sound like_____

I taste like_____

My amazing powers are _____

_____

_____

DRAW YOUR DEMON

Sometimes our problems seem to grow to unbelievable proportions and they begin to take on personalities all their own. The next time you find yourself being intimidated by something that doesn't even have a face (like a situation or an outrageous mess) give it a form and then at least you'll have a physical target for your anger!

When you've met your monster face to face, it won't get to be nearly as monstrous. Try it on this page. Use your imagination and really vent your rage on this paper. It's far better than punching a wall and there is no repair work involved.

"A smile confuses an approaching frown."

----anonymous

THERE'S BAD NEWS AND THERE'S GOOD NEWS

This exercise always helps to put things into proper perspective. There are always two sides to every situation and you may as well focus on the positive! Sit yourself down and write about the situation in a creative and humorous way.

For example, suppose your plumbing springs a leak and you have a kitchen full of water. You might write something like this:

The bad news is that my kitchen is full of water but the good news is that now I have that indoor swimming pool I've always wanted! Now, you try it.

The bad news is: _____

But the good news is: _____

The bad news is: _____

But the good news is: _____

The bad news is: _____

But the good news is: _____

Unpaid Bills   Chocolate Chip Cookies

"The mind in its own place and in itself can make heaven of hell or hell of heaven."

---John Milton

WHAT WOULD YOU SAVE?

Sometimes, in order to get a clear understanding of our priorities, we need to actually verbalize or put them down on paper. This is an eye-opening exercise for you and your students.

If a fire broke out in your home and you only had enough time to gather up three items - people and pets not included - what would you rush to save?

Do this exercise initially with as little thought as possible. Just jot down the first three things that come into your head. Then, upon reflection, try it again and this time, write why you chose those particular items and what that says to you about your priorities.

1. _____
_____
_____
_____
_____

2. _____
_____
_____
_____
_____

3. _____
_____
_____
_____
_____

THINK ABOUT IT:

Chances are, no one wrote that he/she would save his or her garbage! That just wouldn't be one of our priorities. Why, then, are we so intent on hanging on to our emotional garbage (worries, regrets, guilt, grudges, etc.) which clutters our mind and stands in the way of finding true joy and focusing on the what really matters?

DEVELOP YOUR OWN CONTINUING EDUCATION CREDIT WORKSHOPS

Teachers have class. Teachers teach classes. Teachers sit in classes. Every educator is eternally being educated.   Have some fun and get together with some of your coworkers to create some tongue-in-cheek workshop possibilities. Post the list in the lounge and see who signs up!

Here are some examples to get you started:

➢ Holding Your Students' Attention through Intimidation, Fear and Guilt
➢ Whining for Fun and Profit
➢ Burnout and Twitching: How to Make Them Work for You
➢ Teaching Your Students To Talk Good Sos That They Can Get a Gooder Job
➢ Using Halitosis and Body Odor to Reduce Class Size
➢ Guilt without Sex
➢ The Under-Achiever's Guide to Going Nowhere
➢ 101 Creative Uses for Your Stapler
➢ Innovative Ways to Deal with Stress Using a Plunger

Exercise your funny bone and try some of your own:

_____

_____

_____

_____

_____

_____

_____

_____

_____

_____

_____

_____

I TEACH; THEREFORE, I LAUGH

There is not a teacher around who could not make a fortune in a comedy club, telling stories about his or her students. Kids are a rich source of humor and if you're not keeping a journal of funny things they say and do, you're missing a golden opportunity.

Every day offers an abundance of joyous happenings but sometimes we tend to focus on the negative and let the positive go unnoticed. Unfortunately, we tend to have a short memory for the positive things but we will drag the negatives with us forever because we get more sympathy that way.

Break the pattern. Try keeping a joy journal of humorous, touching, uplifting events that happen during your day. Before you go to bed, read the list and reflect on life's little pleasures.

MY **JOY JOURNAL** FOR _____ (today's date)

_____

_____

_____

_____

_____

_____

_____

_____

_____

_____

_____

_____

_____

_____

FOR YOUR FUN FILES: OUT OF THE MOUTHS OF BABES

From the Files of Teachers

> Homer wrote the Oddity.

> An active verb shows action, a passive verb shows passion.

> The future of "I give" is "you take."

> The parts of speech are lungs and air.

> Chicago is nearly at the bottom of Lake Michigan.

> The inhabitants of Moscow are called Mosquitoes.

> A census taker is a man who goes from house to house increasing the population.

> A grasshopper passes through all the life stages from infancy to adultery.

> A triangle which has an angle of 135 degrees is called an obscene triangle.

> Water is composed of two gins. Oxygin and hydrogin. Oxygin is pure gin. Hydrogin is gin and water .

> Feminine hygiene products are America's gross national product.

> Q. What would you do in the case of a person bleeding from a head wound? A. I would tie a tourniquet tightly around his neck.

> Trigonometry is when a lady marries three men at the same time.

> In the Christian religion, a man can have only one wife. This is called monotony.

> In order to be a good nurse, you must be completely sterile.

> In many states with the death penalty, people are put to death by electrolysis.

> Socrates died from an overdose of wedlock.

BACKWORD

Now that you have given yourself and your students a "jump-start" onto the laugh track, you have taken a giant step toward a healthier lifestyle. Whenever you or your students feel the urge to purge yourselves of your worries and woes, make a copy of the following "Whine List" which, unlike the other kind of list which sounds the same, but is spelled differently, is not age restricted. You should write with all your might and vent every frustration you can conjure. Then, take a look at the list, wad it up and flush it down the toilet. With it will go your complaints and you will be free to once more live your life with a laughitude and an "attitude of altitude." Keep laughing - it makes people wonder what you're up to.

MY WHINE LIST

Waaaa, Waaaa, Waaaa...

_____

_____

_____

_____

_____

Furthermore,

_____

_____

_____

_____

_____

_____

Are you finished? Good. Now....................................Go Forth and Laugh!

JUST A TEACHER

Today I was a nurse binding a hurt with the white bandage of compassion,
A doctor healing a small broken world,
A surgeon suturing a friendship together.

Today I was an alchemist seeking gold in base metals,
A scientist answering endless whys,
A philosopher pondering elusive truths.

Today, I was an entertainer, refreshing young minds with laughter,
A fisherman dangling learning as a bait,
A pilot guiding youth away from ignorance.

Today, I was a general campaigning against intolerance,
A lawyer speaking out for brotherhood,
A juror weighing right and wrong.

Today, I was a philanthropist sharing the might of the past,
A mother wholly giving love,
A humble follower of truth.

Mine are such varied occupations.
How can they know me?
Just a teacher.

----author unknown

"What are we going to do?" said Baby Tiger to Mama Tiger in the jungle, "Here comes a
hunter and he has five rifles, three special sighting scopes, and devices
to allow him to see in the dark!"

"Hush!" answered Mama Tiger and she taught her cub how to sneak up from behind and pounce.

The hunter was never heard of again.

All of which goes to prove that technology may be fine,
*but it will never be a substitute for a good **basic education!***

---from 2002 Gems of Educational Wit & Humor

GLOSSARY

ATTITUDE OF ALTITUDE: n. 1. An attitude which elevates one to a place of joy. 2. A way of thinking which allows one to soar with the eagles rather than to run with the turkeys.

BRAIN-BREATHER: n. 1. A mini-recess for the "gray matter." 2. The pause that refreshes. 3. An exercise designed to facilitate in absorbing lessons learned and gearing up for lessons to come.

DELAFFENATED: adj. 1. Refers to the choice to wade and wallow in the wastewater of worldly woe. 2. The opposite of laffenated.

EDUTAIN: v. 1. To educate in an entertaining way.

"FUN"CTIONAL: adj. 1. A term describing a classroom which provides a forum for learning in a variety of ways, including using props, music and games.

GROAN-UP: n. 1. The condition of using one's chronological age as a justification for constantly groaning, moaning, whining, pining and generally feeling sorry for oneself.

HUMORRHOIDS: n. 1. A condition in which the laughter becomes stuck and can't come out; often caused by having one's panties chronically in a bunch. 2. A forerunner of terminal seriousness.

HUMORSCOPE: n. 1. A daily offering on Cybconnect website www.cybconnect.com. 2. Jest the thing to begin the day and provide educators with the mental ammunition to laugh for the health of it. 3. A necessary part of every teacher's daily routine.

LAFFENATED: adj. 1. Refers to the choice to laugh at life, jest for the health of it. 2. The opposite of delaffenated.

LAFFERCISE: n. 1. Exercise for the soul; mental floss. 2. A series of physical actions performed in a silly manner which hopefully will result in the exerciser realizing that creative silliness is a positive condition and prepares one for coping with life's challenges. v. 1. To exercise your funny bones; laughing until you're fit.

LAUGHABLE CLASSROOM: n. 1. A place of educational wonders which celebrates the symbiotic relationship between laughter and learning. 2. A fun place to learn neat stuff.

LAUGHITUDE: n. 1. An attitude of altitude. 2. A way of dealing with life's challenges. 3. What puts a smile on your face and makes you more fun to be around.

MENTAL FLOSS: v. 1. To floss out one's brain, removing the cobwebs of confusion and the nits of negativity.

MIRTHQUAKE: n. 1. An event which results in the participant joyfully quaking with laughter. 2. That which causes the mirthquaker to adjust his or her attitude in preparation for whatever happens.

WHINERAMA: n. 1. A marathon whining contest during which participants complain loudly and whine as if they were made from grapes.

ABOUT THE AUTHOR

Drawing upon her experiences as an Educator, Retirement Counselor, Author, and Trainer, as well as a lifetime in the entertainment business, Linda Henley-Smith provides an amusing and educational outlook on working, living and surviving.

A writer, speaker, and performer, Linda has been featured at conventions, conferences, seminars and special events all across the country and in Europe. She is a trainer in high demand and is currently presenting workshops under her company name of "For The Good Times." Linda's main focus; positive attitude and humor in the workplace, has proven to be a popular topic with schools, medical facilities and corporations of all types. Since the concept is universal, applicable to all fields and an integral part of every organization's plan for success. She is the author of "Lessons in Laughter," "Don't Let Your Fountain Of Youth Get Clogged With The Sands Of Time," and "Adjust Your Attitude and Laugh 'Til the Cows Come Home!"

With more than twenty years experience in the teaching and training field, Linda enjoys speaking to diverse groups and organizations in areas of team building, attitude adjustment, stress management, and the use of humor in challenging situations. She holds a B.A. and M.A. in Education. Linda combines her educational background with her affiliations and experiences in business, the retirement industry, health services, and the arts in order to bring a wide variety of programs, workshops, seminars, and keynotes to all kinds of charitable, educational, and business organizations. In addition, Linda provides training to groups and organizations by implementing innovative activities and projects tailored to each group or organization's needs.

To contact Linda, email her at kitlinda@aol.com or visit her website at www.aybo. com/good-times. To order this book and related products visit the Cyberconnections website at www.cybconnect.com.

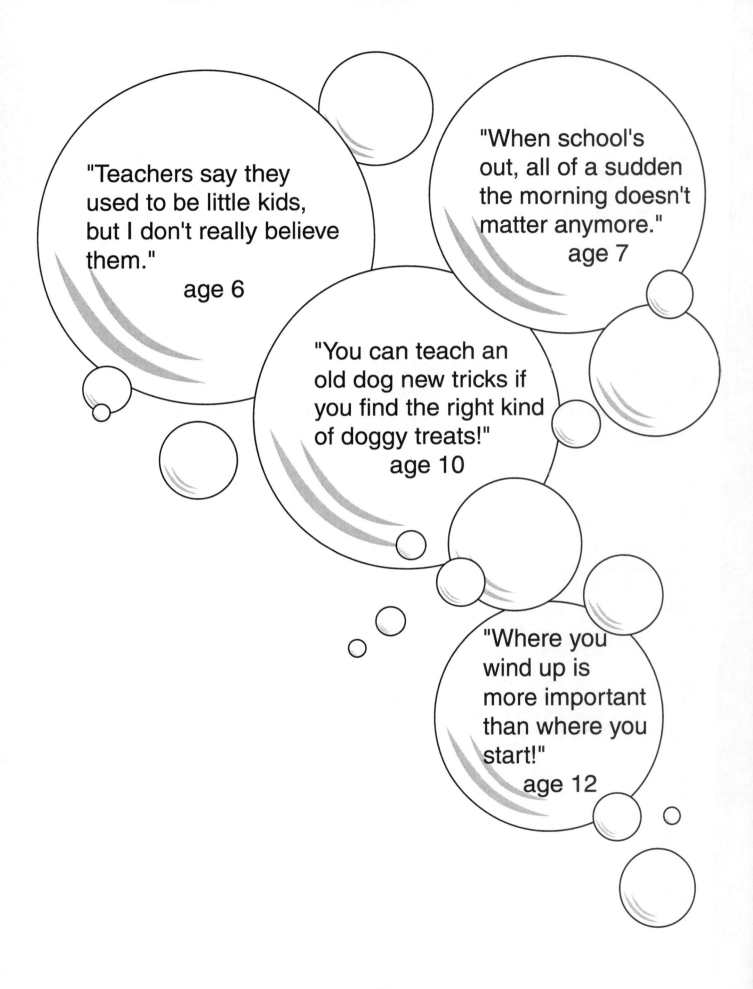

HUMOR ME...I'm a Teacher
By Linda Henley-Smith

To order:
Fax (602) 864-8758 or Mail this completed form.

Number of copies _____ x $19.95 each = $ _____

Shipping & Handling Fee: $3.50

Sales Tax (**AZ only – 7.4%**) $ _____

Total Amount Enclosed: $ _____

Send Money order, personal check, purchase order, or cashier's check (U.S. Funds only)
payable to:

Educational Cyberconnections Inc.
1225 East Broadway, Suite 230
Tempe, AZ 85282

Method of Payment

Purchase order number: _____

Check number: _____

Type of credit card: _____

Name on credit card: _____

Credit card number: _____

Expiration date: (mm/yyyy) _____

Today's Date: _____/_____/_____.

Ship to (Name): _____

Title: _____ Organization: _____

Address: _____

City: _____ State: _____ Zip Code: _____

Daytime Phone: _____ Fax: _____

Email: _____

Please allow 3 to 5 weeks for delivery

For information about your order, call toll-free (888) 923-8400 or email us at: info @cybconnect.com

Call for DISCOUNTS on quantity orders!

Check out our web site for other products from ECI:
http://www.cybconnect.com